CRC　　　　3/2　　　　　　　1·00

THE BOOK OF

CURRIES
&
INDIAN FOODS

INTRODUCTION

Indian food is rich and varied; it includes many regional cooking styles – each highly distinctive, but all equally delicious.

The Book of Curries & Indian Foods dips into all the regions to bring you over 100 recipes – all beautifully illustrated in colour with step-by-step instructions. Discover how to transform everyday foods into exotic dishes – from the well known Chicken Tikka to Sole with Dill Stuffing and Golden Steamed Chicken.

You'll discover the rich variety of Indian vegetable dishes, too. Ordinary vegetables are transformed when combined with wonderful spices and delicious sauces.

Find out the secrets of Indian breads like Chapati and Naan – there are easy to follow recipes with step-by-step instructions to make them so simple to prepare.

You will find that not all Indian food is hot – there are mouthwatering salads, fresh chutneys and fabulous, irresistible desserts, such as Fritters & Fragrant Syrup and Pistachio Halva, that are sweet and delicately scented, as well as cooling fruity summer drinks like Lime & Mint Sherbet and Indian Summer Punch.

When you try the recipes, remember that they are only meant as a basic guide – add a pinch of extra spice here, omit the chillies there or add an extra ingredient if you like. It's your personal touch -- what Indians call 'Hath ki bat' – that makes all the difference!

— THE CULTURAL INFLUENCES —

Indian food encompasses the cooking of many different regions – the country itself is huge, over a million square miles – and the foods are quite different from state to state.

In the north, where the climate is temperate, sheep are reared – and the lamb dishes are generally cooked slowly in the oven. Travelling south through Delhi and the Punjab, the diet becomes much richer – here they cook mainly with ghee (a clarified butter) and eat both goat and chicken. In these northern regions, instead of rice, the preference is for breads.

To the east, around the Bay of Bengal, there is an abundance of fish from the many rivers and, of course, from the bay itself. Coconut palms grow in the hot and humid climate, so coconuts feature strongly in many of their recipes. On the west coast, in Gujarat, the people are mainly vegetarian, eating pulses and vegetables, and in Tamil Nadu in the far south east, the people are also vegetarian.

The humid tropical conditions of the south west, in Goa and Malabar, mean that date and coconut palms, and banana plants flourish and here there is also plenty of fish and shellfish. Southern Indians eat more rice than the northerners and they prefer to steam foods – the dishes are traditionally very hot, much more so than in the north. However, the story doesn't end there.

Influence of race and religion
India is a country of vastly varied races and religions – and it is religion that influences diet to the greatest extent. There are hundreds of different religions, some original, others imported over the centuries by conquering peoples from other lands, each with its own customs and taboos. For instance, Moslems and Jews don't eat pork, while Hindus and Sikhs are prohibited from eating beef, and although many Hindus are strict vegetarians, others eat fish and shellfish, classing these as a harvest from the seas.

Use of spices
The imaginative use of spices sets Indian cooking apart from other cuisines – it is by far the most aromatic of

all types of cooking – and perhaps the most pleasant discovery one can make about it is that although always spicy, the food isn't necessarily hot. In fact chillies – which make the food hot – were only introduced to India in the 16th century by Portuguese traders.

Red chillies are usually hotter than green and larger chillies generally milder than small ones, and unless you like very hot food, the seeds of all types are best removed. Be careful when handling the chillies, they contain an irritant which can burn, especially tender areas like the eyes and mouth. Try not to touch the seeds or cut surfaces of the chillies and always wash your hands afterwards.

Other spices can add warmth in different degrees – mustard seeds, black pepper and cayenne pepper are all quite hot, while ground ginger, nutmeg and cardamom are warm. Whole spices are best removed from dishes before serving.

The cornerstone of Indian cooking is the spice mixtures – or masalas. Spices release their flavour when they are crushed and traditionally spices are ground by hand on a hard grinding stone with a pestle. At home, a mortar and pestle works very well for small quantities. However, if you have an electric coffee grinder, you will be able to make light work of spice grinding.

The most common spices are cumin, coriander and mustard seeds, black pepper, ground turmeric, cinnamon, cardamom and cloves. It's worth going to a specialist shop to buy whole spices rather than using the ready-ground ones as the whole spices have a stronger flavour which lasts much longer. Buy small quantities and store them in an airtight container.

Fats
The fats traditionally used in Indian cooking are ghee (a clarified butter) and solid vegetable fat. Until recently in Northern India ghee was the only fat used, however, there is a growing awareness about healthy eating and many Indians are swapping to vegetable fat. I have used vegetable oil in most of the recipes and have generally reduced fat quantities where I felt it would improve the taste of the recipe.

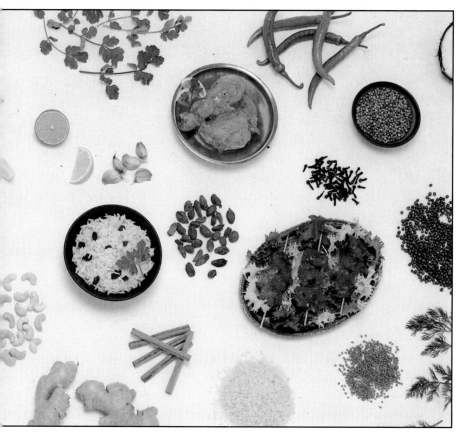

SPICE MIXES & COCONUT MILK

NUT MASALA

2 tablespoons vegetable oil
1 teaspoon cumin seeds
1 teaspoon cardamom seeds
3 teaspoons poppy seeds
1 teaspoon black peppercorns
2 cloves garlic, crushed
2.5 cm (1 in) piece fresh root ginger, grated
60 g (2 oz/⅓ cup) blanched almonds or unsalted
    cashew nuts, chopped
75 ml (2½ fl oz/⅓ cup) boiling water

Heat oil in a heavy-based frying pan, add spices and fry over a medium heat for 5-10 minutes, until golden brown, stirring constantly. Add garlic and ginger and cook for 2 minutes more, then leave to cool. Put spice mixture in a blender or food processor fitted with a metal blade. Add almonds or cashew nuts and water and grind to a smooth paste. Cover tightly and keep in a cool place for up to 1 week.

TANDOORI MASALA

3 teaspoons cumin seeds
3 teaspoons coriander seeds
3 teaspoons cayenne pepper
few drops red food colouring

Grind cumin and coriander seeds using a coffee grinder or pestle and mortar. Stir in cayenne pepper and food colouring and mix well. Store in a small, airtight jar for up to 2 months.

MURGHAL MASALA

seeds from 60 g (2 oz) green cardamom pods
two 7.5 cm (3 in) cinnamon sticks, crushed
3 teaspoons whole cloves
3 teaspoons black peppercorns
1 teaspoon grated nutmeg

Grind spices to a fine powder using a coffee grinder or pestle and mortar. Store in a small, airtight jar for up to 2 months.

GARAM MASALA

4 teaspoons cardamom seeds
two 7.5 cm (3 in) cinnamon sticks, crushed
2 teaspoons whole cloves
4 teaspoons black peppercorns
3 tablespoons cumin seeds
3 tablespoons coriander seeds

Put spices in a heavy-based frying pan and fry over medium heat for 5-10 minutes, until browned, stirring. Cool, then grind to a fine powder. Store for up to 2 months.

HOT SPICE MIX

4 tablespoons cumin seeds
8 dried red chillies
3 teaspoons black peppercorns
3 teaspoons cardamom seeds
7.5 cm (3 in) cinnamon stick, crushed
4 teaspoons black mustard seeds
3 teaspoons fenugreek seeds

Prepare as for Garam Masala (above). Store in an airtight jar for up to 2 months.

COCONUT MILK

100 g (3½ oz/1 cup) desiccated, fresh or creamed coconut
500 ml (16 fl oz/2 cups) hot water

Put coconut and water in a blender or food processor fitted with a metal blade; process for 1 minute. Strain through a nylon sieve, squeezing out liquid, then discard coconut. (There is no need to sieve creamed coconut.)

Makes about 500 ml (16 fl oz/2 cups).

MURGHAL MASALA CHOPS

8 best end-of-neck lamb chops
3 teaspoons Murghal Masala, see page 11
¼ teaspoon chilli powder
1 clove garlic, crushed
3 teaspoons lemon juice
curly endive and cherry tomatoes, to garnish

Wipe lamb chops and trim off any excess fat. Slash meaty parts 2 or 3 times on each side and set aside.

Put murghal masala, chilli powder, garlic and lemon juice in a small bowl and mix to a smooth paste. Rub paste into chops and leave them in a cool place for 2-3 hours to allow meat to absorb flavours.

Heat grill. Place chops on a grill rack and cook for 12-15 minutes, turning over half-way through cooking, until browned on outsides and just pink in centres. Press point of a sharp knife into centres of chops – when they are ready, juices will be just faintly pink. Serve hot, garnished with curly endive and tomatoes.

Serves 4.

—— SKEWERED BEEF KEBABS ——

750 g (1½ lb) lean minced beef
1 onion, finely chopped
5 cm (2 in) piece fresh root ginger, grated
3 cloves garlic, crushed
1 teaspoon chilli powder
3 teaspoons Garam Masala, see page 11
1 tablespoon chopped fresh coriander
3 teaspoons ground almonds
1 egg, beaten
30 g (1 oz/¼ cup) chick-pea flour
6 tablespoons natural yogurt
2 teaspoons vegetable oil
raw onion rings and thin lemon wedges, to garnish

In a large bowl, mix beef, onion, ginger, garlic, chilli powder, garam masala, coriander, almonds, egg and flour together. Cover beef mixture and leave in a cool place for up to 4 hours to allow flavours to blend. Shape into 16-20 long ovals and thread onto 4 long skewers. Mix together yogurt and oil and brush over kebabs.

Heat grill. Cook kebabs for 20-25 minutes, until well browned and no longer pink in centres. Baste kebabs with more of the yogurt and oil mixture and turn occasionally during cooking. Serve hot, garnished with onion rings and lemon wedges.

Serves 4.

Note: The meatball mixture can be made up to 12 hours in advance and stored in a refrigerator.

LAMB TIKKA

1 kg (2 lb) boneless leg of lamb
1 teaspoon ground cumin
¾ teaspoon turmeric
salt
6 tablespoons natural yogurt
½ small onion, finely chopped
5 cm (2 in) piece fresh root ginger, grated
2 cloves garlic, crushed
few drops red food colouring, optional
1 teaspoon Garam Masala, see page 11

Trim fat from lamb and cut lamb into 4 cm (1½ in) cubes. Put lamb in a bowl and add cumin, turmeric, salt, yogurt, onion, ginger and garlic.

Mix together well, then, if you wish, add enough colouring to give mixture a red tinge. Cover and leave in refrigerator for 4-6 hours to marinate. Drain lamb from marinade and thread cubes onto 8 short skewers, pressing cubes closely together.

Heat grill. Cook kebabs for 15-20 minutes, basting kebabs with any remaining marinade and turning occasionally during cooking, until well browned and done to taste. Sprinkle with garam masala and serve at once.

Serves 4.

Note: These kebabs can be cooked on a barbecue using metal skewers. Cooking time depends on heat of barbecue.

— KASHMIR MEATBALL CURRY —

750 g (1½ lb) minced lamb
30 g (1 oz/¼ cup) chick-pea flour
9 teaspoons Garam Masala, see page 11
¼ teaspoon cayenne pepper
6 tablespoons natural yogurt
salt
2 tablespoons vegetable oil
7.5 cm (3 in) cinnamon stick
6 green cardamom pods, bruised
2 fresh bay leaves
6 whole cloves
5 cm (2 in) piece fresh root ginger, grated
2 tablespoons chopped fresh coriander, to garnish

Put lamb, flour, garam masala, cayenne and half the yogurt in a bowl. Season with salt and mix together well. Shape into 16 long ovals. Heat oil in a shallow heavy-based pan, add cinnamon, cardamom pods, bay leaves and cloves. Stir-fry for a few seconds, then add meatballs and fry until lightly browned on all sides. Add ginger and fry for a few seconds more. Stir remaining yogurt into 250 ml (8 fl oz/1 cup) cold water and pour over meatballs.

Cover pan and bring to the boil. Reduce heat and simmer for about 30 minutes, stirring gently 2 or 3 times, until meatballs are cooked and almost all the sauce has been absorbed. Sprinkle with coriander and serve at once.

Serves 4.

Note: If meatballs release a lot of fat during initial frying, drain it off before adding yogurt liquid.

— HOT & SOUR PORK CURRY —

750 g (1½ lb) boneless shoulder of pork
6 tablespoons vegetable oil
2 onions, finely sliced
9 teaspoons Hot Spice Mix, see page 11
60 ml (2 fl oz/¼ cup) white wine vinegar
1 teaspoon soft brown sugar
2.5 cm (1 in) piece fresh root ginger, grated
6 cloves garlic, crushed
1 teaspoon turmeric
1 teaspoon paprika
1 teaspoon ground coriander
red chilli flower, to garnish

Wipe the pork and cut into 2.5 cm (1 in) cubes.

Heat half the oil in a heavy-based pan, add onions and cook for 10 minutes or until brown and crisp, stirring constantly. Remove with a slotted spoon and set aside. Mix together hot spice mix, vinegar, sugar, ginger, garlic, turmeric, paprika and coriander, blending to a smooth paste. Add remaining oil to pan and fry pork until lightly browned, then remove with a slotted spoon and set aside.

Add spice mixture to pan and cook, stirring, for 2-3 minutes. Return meat and any juices to pan. Stir in 250 ml (8 fl oz/1 cup) water, and bring to the boil, then simmer, covered, for 45 minutes. Stir in three-quarters of the onion and cook for a further 15-30 minutes, until pork is tender and cooked through. Serve hot, garnished with remaining onions and chilli flower.

Serves 4.

– RED LAMB & ALMOND CURRY –

750 g (1½ lb) boneless leg of lamb
60 ml (2 fl oz/¼ cup) vegetable oil
6 green cardamom pods, bruised
1 teaspoon turmeric
1 teaspoon chilli powder
1 teaspoon ground cumin
3 teaspoons paprika
1 teaspoon ground coriander
1 small piece rattan jog (type of bark which stains food
    red), optional
1 quantity Almond Masala, see page 10
155 ml (5 fl oz/⅔ cup) natural yogurt
440 g (14 oz) can chopped tomatoes
1 large onion, finely chopped

Trim excess fat from lamb and cut lamb into
4 cm (1½ in) cubes. Heat oil in a heavy-
based pan, add cardamoms, turmeric, chilli
powder, cumin, paprika, coriander, rattan
jog, if using, and masala. Fry, stirring, for 2-
3 minutes, then stir in yogurt and tomatoes
and bring to the boil. Add onion and cook
for 3-4 minutes. Add lamb cubes, stir well
and cover.

Bring to the boil again, then reduce heat
and cook for 40-50 minutes, until lamb is
tender and liquid makes a thick sauce,
stirring occasionally.

Serves 4.

Note: On special occasions, this dish can be
garnished with real silver leaf from Indian
shops. Just before serving, place a sheet,
silver side down, on top and peel off backing
paper.

LAMB KORMA

750 g (1½ lb) boneless leg of lamb
60 ml (2 fl oz/¼ cup) vegetable oil
1 large onion, finely chopped
1 quantity Cashew Nut Masala, see page 10
6 teaspoons Garam Masala, see page 11
3 dried red chillies, seeded and crushed
2.5 cm (1 in) piece fresh root ginger, grated
1 tablespoon chopped fresh coriander
250 ml (8 fl oz/1 cup) single (light) cream
salt
2 teaspoons lemon juice
coriander leaves and lemon wedges, to garnish

Wipe lamb, trim off excess fat and cut into 5 cm (2 in) cubes.

Heat oil in a heavy-based pan, add lamb and fry until browned all over. Add onion and cook for about 5 minutes, stirring frequently, until soft. Stir in masalas, chillies and ginger and cook for 2 minutes more.

Add chopped coriander, cream and 75 ml (2½ fl oz/⅓ cup) water and season with salt. Bring to the boil and simmer, covered, for about 1 hour or until lamb is tender. Stir in lemon juice and serve hot, garnished with coriander and lemon wedges.

Serves 4.

MADRAS MEAT CURRY

750 g (1½ lb) braising steak
6 teaspoons vegetable oil
1 large onion, finely sliced
4 cloves
4 green cardamom pods, bruised
3 fresh green chillies, seeded and finely chopped
2 dry red chillies, seeded and crushed
2.5 cm (1 in) piece fresh root ginger, grated
2 cloves garlic, crushed
2 teaspoons ground coriander
2 teaspoons turmeric
60 ml (2 fl oz/¼ cup) tamarind juice, see Note
salt
lettuce leaves, to garnish

Cut beef into 2.5 cm (1 in) cubes. Heat oil in a large heavy-based pan, add beef and fry until browned all over. Remove with a slotted spoon and set aside. Add onion, cloves and cardamom pods to pan and fry for about 8 minutes, stirring, until onion is soft and golden brown. Stir in chillies, ginger, garlic, coriander and turmeric and fry for 2 minutes. Return beef to pan, add 60 ml (2 fl oz/¼ cup) water and simmer, covered, for 1 hour.

Stir in tamarind juice and season with salt, re-cover and simmer, covered, for 15-30 minutes, until beef is tender. Serve garnished with lettuce leaves.

Serves 4.

Note: Tamarind pulp, available in Indian shops, is used to make tamarind juice. Soak walnut-sized piece in 250 ml (8 fl oz/1 cup) boiling water for 20 minutes, then squeeze pulp in muslin to extract juice; discard pulp.

MINTY LAMB PATTIES

60 g (2 oz/⅓ cup) whole brown lentils
315 ml (10 fl oz/1¼ cups) boiling water
3 onions, finely chopped
500 g (1 lb) minced lamb
6 teaspoons Garam Masala, see page 11
2 dried red chillies, seeded and crushed
1 egg, beaten
60 ml (2 fl oz/¼ cup) natural yogurt
2 tablespoons chopped fresh mint
2 fresh green chillies, seeded and chopped
60 ml (2 fl oz/¼ cup) vegetable oil
fresh mint leaves, to garnish

Put lentils in a bowl, add water and leave to soak for 2 hours.

Put lentils, their soaking water, 2 onions, lamb, garam masala and red chillies in a large heavy-based pan and bring to the boil. Cook, uncovered, over a medium heat, stirring constantly, until all the liquid has evaporated and mixture is very dry. Remove from heat and leave to cool. Put mixture in a blender or food processor fitted with a metal blade and process to a smooth paste. Add egg and yogurt and blend again. Chill for 2-3 hours, then form into 16 balls.

Mix together remaining onion, mint and green chillies. Make an indentation in each lamb ball and stuff with a little minty mixture, then cover up with meat. Flatten balls into 5 cm (2in) patties. Heat oil in a frying pan and fry patties a few at a time for 4-6 minutes, turning over after half the time, until well browned. Serve, garnished with fresh mint leaves.

Serves 4.

— LEG OF LAMB & PISTACHIOS —

1.75-2 kg (3½-4 lb) leg of lamb, boned, rolled
   and tied
2 cloves garlic, crushed
2.5 cm (1 in) piece fresh root ginger, grated
1 teaspoon ground cumin
2 teaspoons Murghal Masala, see page 11
salt and cayenne pepper
125 g (4 oz/¾ cup) shelled pistachio nuts
6 teaspoons lemon juice
6 teaspoons soft brown sugar
125 ml (4 fl oz/½ cup) natural yogurt
2 pinches saffron threads
6 teaspoons boiling water
3 teaspoons cornflour
2 tablespoons shelled pistachio nuts, sliced, to garnish

Prick lamb all over with point of a knife and place in a large glass bowl. Put garlic, ginger, cumin, masala, salt and cayenne pepper to taste, pistachio nuts, lemon juice, sugar and yogurt in a blender or food processor fitted with a metal blade and process until smooth. Pour over lamb and leave to marinate for 24 hours, turning lamb occasionally. Preheat oven to 180C (350F/Gas 4). Transfer lamb to a flameproof casserole, add 155 ml (5 fl oz/⅔ cup) water and bring to the boil.

Cover tightly and cook in oven for 1½ hours. Reduce heat to 140C (275F/Gas 1) and cook for 30 minutes. Turn off oven and leave for 30 minutes. Soak saffron in water for 20 minutes, then blend in cornflour. Remove lamb and keep warm. Skim excess fat from sauce, add saffron mixture and boil, stirring, until thick. Slice lamb, pour a little sauce over; garnish with nuts. Serve rest of sauce separately.

Serves 6-8.

BEEF-STUFFED CABBAGE

2 onions
5 tablespoons vegetable oil
3 cloves garlic, crushed
2 fresh green chillies, seeded and chopped
7.5 cm (3 in) piece fresh root ginger, grated
500 g (1 lb) lean minced beef
¼ teaspoon turmeric
2 teaspoons Garam Masala, see page 11
1 savoy cabbage
440 g (14 oz) can chopped tomatoes
6 teaspoons lemon juice
salt and pepper
lemon or lime slices, to garnish

Chop 1 onion and slice the other.

Heat 2 tablespoons oil in a heavy-based pan, add chopped onion and cook over a medium heat, stirring, for about 8 minutes, until soft and golden brown. Add garlic, chillies and one-third of the ginger and cook for 1 minute, then remove with a slotted spoon and set aside.

Add beef to pan and cook, stirring, until browned and well broken up. Stir in turmeric and garam masala and cook for 1 minute, then add onion mixture.

Cook, covered, for 20-30 minutes, stirring occasionally, until cooking liquid is absorbed. Leave to cool. Remove core from cabbage with a sharp knife. Cook whole cabbage in boiling salted water for 8 minutes, then drain and rinse in cold water. Leave until cool enough to handle, then carefully peel off 12-16 outside leaves, keeping them whole. Finely shred remaining cabbage.

To make sauce, heat remaining oil in a heavy-based pan, add sliced onion and cook, stirring frequently, for 5 minutes or until soft but not brown. Add shredded cabbage, tomatoes, remaining ginger, lemon juice and 155ml (5 fl oz/⅔ cup) water. Season with salt and pepper. Bring to the boil, then simmer, uncovered, for 5 minutes.

Preheat oven to 190C (375F/Gas 5). Put about 2 tablespoons mince mixture on each cabbage leaf, fold sides in and roll up neatly. Pour a little sauce into base of an ovenproof casserole, add cabbage rolls and pour over remaining sauce. Cover and cook for 40-50 minutes, until cabbage is tender. Serve hot, garnished with lemon or lime slices.

Serves 4.

LAMB WITH ONIONS

750 g (1½ lb) shoulder of lamb, boned
1 teaspoon turmeric
1 teaspoon ground cumin
1 teaspoon ground coriander
2.5 cm (1 in) piece fresh root ginger, grated
2 cloves garlic, crushed
45 ml (1½ fl oz/9 teaspoons) vegetable oil
3 teaspoons caster sugar
4 large onions, sliced into thin rings
500 g (1 lb) potatoes, cut into large chunks
salt and cayenne pepper
1 teaspoon Garam Masala, see page 11
rosemary sprigs, to garnish

Wipe lamb, trim and cut into cubes.

Put lamb in a glass or china bowl. Mix together turmeric, cumin, coriander, ginger and garlic and add to lamb. Stir well, then cover loosely and leave in a cool place for 2-3 hours. Heat oil in heavy-based pan until smoking. Stir in sugar, then add onions and cook over a medium to high heat for 10 minutes, stirring frequently, until a rich brown. Remove onions with a slotted spoon and set aside.

Add lamb to pan and fry until browned all over. Add potatoes and fry, stirring, for 2 minutes. Return onions to pan, add 250 ml (8 fl oz/1 cup) water and season with salt and cayenne pepper. Bring to the boil and simmer, covered, for 1¼ hours, or until lamb is tender, stirring occasionally. Stir in garam masala and serve, garnished with rosemary sprigs.

Serves 4.

SPICY SPARE RIBS

1-1.25 kg (2-2½ lb) meaty pork spare ribs
9 teaspoons Hot Spice Mix, see page 11
1 teaspoon turmeric
5 cm (2 in) piece fresh root ginger, grated
1 small onion, finely chopped
3 teaspoons white wine vinegar
3 teaspoons tomato purée (paste)
spring onions and tomatoes, to garnish

Cut ribs into single rib pieces and chop into 7.5 cm (3 in) lengths.

Place ribs in a large saucepan, cover with cold water and bring to the boil, then simmer for 15 minutes. Drain. Put hot spice mix, turmeric, ginger, onion, vinegar and tomato purée (paste) in a blender or food processor fitted with a metal blade. Add 75 ml (2½ fl oz/⅓ cup) water and process until smooth.

Place ribs in a non-metal dish, pour over spice mixture and stir to coat well. Cover loosely and leave in a cool place for 2-3 hours. Transfer ribs to a grill pan. Heat grill. Cook ribs for about 15 minutes, turning occasionally and basting with any remaining marinade, until well browned and very tender. Serve hot, garnished with spring onions and tomatoes.

Serves 4.

PORK IN SPINACH SAUCE

750 g (1½ lb) fresh spinach, well rinsed
salt
750 g (1½ lb) lean boneless pork
3 tablespoons vegetable oil
2 onions, finely sliced
4 cloves garlic, crushed
2.5 cm (1 in) piece fresh root ginger, grated
9 teaspoons Garam Masala, see page 11
½ teaspoon turmeric
1 bay leaf
2 tomatoes, skinned and chopped
2 fresh green chillies, seeded and chopped
155 ml (5 fl oz/⅔ cup) natural yogurt
tomato slices and bay leaves, to garnish

Trim stems from spinach and cook leaves in boiling salted water for 2-3 minutes, until tender. Drain thoroughly and rinse under cold running water. Put in a blender or food processor fitted with a metal blade and process to a smooth purée. Set aside. Pre-heat oven to 160C (325F/Gas 3). Cut pork into 2.5 cm (1 in) cubes. Heat oil in a large frying pan and fry pork until browned all over. Transfer to a casserole using a slotted spoon.

Add onions to pan and cook, stirring, for 10-15 minutes, until a rich brown. Add garlic, ginger, garam masala, turmeric, bay leaf, tomatoes and chillies. Cook, stirring, for 2-3 minutes, until tomatoes have softened. Add yogurt and 155 ml (5 fl oz/⅔ cup) water and stir. Pour over pork, cover and cook for 1¼-1½ hours, until pork is cooked through. Remove bay leaf, stir in spinach and salt, re-cover and cook for a further 10 minutes. Garnish and serve.

Serves 4.

— LAMB WITH CAULIFLOWER —

750 g (1½ lb) lamb fillet
3 tablespoons vegetable oil
2 onions, finely chopped
2.5 cm (1 in) piece fresh root ginger, grated
4 cloves garlic, crushed
6 teaspoons Hot Spice Mix, see page 11
315 ml (10 fl oz/1¼ cups) lamb stock
salt
1 small cauliflower, cut into flowerets
1 teaspoon Garam Masala, see page 11
2 teaspoons lime juice
lime slices, to garnish

Trim excess fat from lamb and cut into 2.5 cm (1 in) cubes. Set aside.

Heat oil in a large heavy-based pan and add onions. Fry over a medium heat for 5 minutes, stirring frequently, until soft. Stir in ginger, garlic and hot spice mix and fry for 1 minute. Add lamb and fry until browned all over.

Stir in stock, season with salt and bring to the boil, then simmer, covered, for 25 minutes. Add cauliflower and cook for a further 5-10 minutes, stirring occasionally, until lamb and cauliflower are tender. Sprinkle in garam masala and lime juice and stir gently. Serve the lamb hot, garnished with thin lime slices.

Serves 4.

CHICKEN IN GINGER SAUCE

four 185 g (6 oz) boneless chicken breasts (fillets),
   skinned
2 tablespoons vegetable oil
6 spring onions, finely chopped
3 cloves garlic, crushed
5 cm (2 in) piece fresh root ginger, grated
1 teaspoon ground cumin
2 teaspoons Garam Masala, see page 11
salt and pepper
3 teaspoons lemon juice
6 tablespoons hot water
parsley sprigs and lemon slices, to garnish

Wash chicken, pat dry with absorbent kitchen paper and slice thinly.

Heat oil in a large frying pan, add onions and fry for 2-3 minutes, stirring, to soften. Remove from pan with a slotted spoon. Put chicken in pan and fry over a high heat, stirring frequently, for about 5 minutes or until browned all over.

Stir in garlic, ginger, cumin and garam masala and season with salt and pepper. Cook for 1 minute, then stir in onions, lemon juice and water. Cover and cook over a low heat for about 10 minutes or until chicken is tender. Serve hot, garnished with parsley and lemon.

Serves 4.

ROAST DUCK IN FRUIT SAUCE

2.25 kg (4½ lb) duck
3 onions, chopped
125 g (4 oz/1 cup) chopped mixed nuts
60 g (2 oz/1 cup) fresh breadcrumbs
4 tablespoons chopped fresh coriander
salt and cayenne pepper
1 egg yolk
3 teaspoons Garam Masala, see page 11
2 tablespoons vegetable oil
2 garlic cloves, crushed
2.5 cm (1 in) piece fresh root ginger, grated
1 teaspoon turmeric
6 teaspoons ground coriander
1 teaspoon chick-pea flour
315 ml (10 fl oz/1¼ cups) natural yogurt
juice of 2 lemons and 2 oranges

Preheat oven to 190C (375F/Gas 5). Wash
duck and pat dry with absorbent kitchen
paper, then prick skin with a fork. In a bowl,
mix 1 onion, nuts, breadcrumbs, 3 tablespoons fresh coriander, salt and cayenne
pepper and yolk together. Use to stuff duck,
then truss neatly. Rub garam masala into
skin, place duck in a roasting tin and cook
for 1¼ hours or until tender. Remove duck
and keep warm. Heat oil in a saucepan, add
remaining onions and cook, stirring, for 5
minutes, until soft.

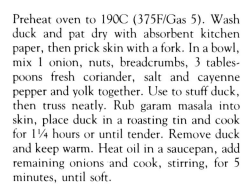

Stir in garlic, ginger, turmeric, ground
coriander, salt and cayenne pepper to taste
and flour. Cook for 1 minute, then stir in
yogurt. Simmer for 10 minutes, then stir in
lemon and orange juices and heat gently,
without boiling. Carve duck, pour over
sauce and sprinkle with remaining coriander. Serve hot.

Serves 4.

Note: This looks very attractive garnished
with spirals of lemon and orange peel.

LEMON & CORIANDER CHICKEN

4 chicken thighs, skinned
4 chicken drumsticks, skinned
60 ml (2 fl oz/¼ cup) vegetable oil
5 cm (2 in) piece fresh root ginger, grated
4 cloves garlic, crushed
1 fresh green chilli, seeded and finely chopped
½ teaspoon turmeric
1 teaspoon ground cumin
1 teaspoon ground coriander
salt and cayenne pepper
grated peel and juice of 1 lemon
125 g (4 oz) fresh coriander leaves, chopped
coriander leaves and lemon slices, to garnish

Wash chicken joints and pat dry with absorbent kitchen paper. Heat oil in a large frying pan, add chicken, and fry, stirring frequently, until browned all over. Remove from pan with a slotted spoon and set aside. Add ginger and garlic to pan and fry for 1 minute. Stir in chilli, turmeric, cumin and ground coriander and season with salt and cayenne pepper, then cook for 1 minute more.

Return chicken to pan, add 125 ml (4 fl oz/½ cup) water and lemon peel and juice. Bring to the boil, then cover and cook over a medium heat for 25-30 minutes or until chicken is tender. Stir in chopped coriander, then serve hot, garnished with fresh coriander leaves and lemon slices.

Serves 4.

Variation: Use fresh parsley, or parsley and mint, instead of coriander, if preferred.

APRICOT & CHICKEN CURRY

1.25 kg (2½ lb) chicken joints, skinned
½ teaspoon chilli powder
3 teaspoons Garam Masala, see page 11
2.5 cm (1 in) piece fresh root ginger, grated
2 cloves garlic, crushed
125 g (4 oz/1 cup) ready-to-eat dried apricots
2 tablespoons vegetable oil
2 onions, finely sliced
440 g (14 oz) can chopped tomatoes
3 teaspoons sugar
6 teaspoons white wine vinegar
salt

Wash chicken and pat dry with absorbent kitchen paper. Cut each joint into 4 pieces and put in a large bowl. Add chilli powder, garam masala, ginger and garlic and toss well to coat chicken pieces. Cover and leave in a cool place for 2-3 hours, to allow chicken to absorb flavours. In a separate bowl, put apricots and 155 ml (5 fl oz/⅔ cup) water and leave to soak for 2-3 hours.

Heat oil in a large heavy-based pan and add chicken. Fry over a high heat for 5 minutes or until browned all over. Remove from pan and set aside. Add onions to pan and cook, stirring, for about 5 minutes, until soft. Return chicken to pan with tomatoes and cook, covered, over a low heat for 20 minutes. Drain apricots, add to pan with sugar and vinegar. Season with salt. Simmer, covered, for 10-15 minutes. Serve hot.

Serves 4.

TANDOORI CHICKEN

1.25 kg (2½ lb) chicken joints, skinned
3 teaspoons lime juice
salt
1 small onion
3 teaspoons Tandoori Masala, see page 10
2 teaspoons Garam Masala, see page 11
2.5 cm (1 in) piece fresh root ginger, grated
315 ml (10 fl oz/1¼ cups) natural yogurt
lime wedges and coriander leaves, to garnish

Wash chicken joints and pat dry with absorbent kitchen paper, then slash meaty parts 2 or 3 times.

Place chicken in a shallow non-metal dish. Sprinkle with lime juice and salt and set aside. Put onion, masalas, ginger, salt and yogurt into a blender or food processor fitted with a metal blade and process until smooth and frothy. Pour over chicken and cover loosely. Leave to marinate in a cool place for 6 hours or overnight.

Preheat oven to 200C (400F/Gas 6). Drain excess marinade from chicken joints and place them in a roasting tin. Cook for 25-30 minutes, until tender and well browned. Serve hot, garnished with lime wedges and coriander leaves.

Serves 4.

Note: If preferred, use a whole 1.5 kg (3 lb) roasting chicken and cook for 1¼-1½ hours or until juices run clear.

SPICY CHICKEN PATTIES

625 g (1¼ lb) boneless chicken breasts (fillets), skinned
90 g (3 oz/1½ cups) fresh breadcrumbs
4 spring onions, finely chopped
3 tomatoes, skinned, seeded and chopped
3 tablespoons chopped fresh coriander
2.5 cm (1 in) piece fresh root ginger, grated
1 clove garlic, crushed
1 teaspoon ground cumin
1 teaspoon Garam Masala, see page 11
salt and cayenne pepper
1 egg, beaten
60 ml (2 fl oz/¼ cup) vegetable oil
tomato wedges and spring onion tassels, to garnish

Wash chicken breasts (fillets) and pat dry with absorbent kitchen paper. Finely mince chicken and put into a large bowl with half the breadcrumbs and the onions, tomatoes, coriander, ginger, garlic, cumin, garam masala, salt and cayenne pepper to taste, and egg. Mix thoroughly, then divide into 18 pieces and form into patties. Roll patties in remaining breadcrumbs to coat all over.

Heat oil in a large frying pan. Fry patties in 2 or 3 batches for 10-12 minutes, until crisp and golden brown on both sides and no longer pink in centres. Drain on absorbent kitchen paper. Serve hot, garnished with tomato wedges and spring onion tassels.

Serves 6.

Note: Patties can be prepared up to 12 hours in advance and chilled.

DUCK & COCONUT CURRY

4 duck portions, skinned
2 tablespoons vegetable oil
1 teaspoon mustard seeds
1 onion, finely chopped
3 cloves garlic, crushed
5 cm (2 in) piece fresh root ginger, grated
2 fresh green chillies, seeded and chopped
1 teaspoon ground cumin
3 teaspoons ground coriander
1 teaspoon turmeric
3 teaspoons white wine vinegar
salt and cayenne pepper
315 ml (10 fl oz/1¼ cups) Coconut Milk, see page 11
2 tablespoons shredded coconut, toasted, and lemon
    wedges, to garnish

Wash duck and pat dry with absorbent kitchen paper. Heat oil in a large frying pan, add duck and fry, stirring, over a high heat for 8-10 minutes, until browned all over, then remove from pan. Pour off all but 2 tablespoons fat from pan, add mustard seeds and fry for 1 minute or until they begin to pop.

Add onion to pan and cook, stirring, over a medium heat for 8 minutes or until soft and golden. Stir in garlic, ginger, chillies, cumin, coriander and turmeric and fry for 2 minutes. Stir in vinegar and season with salt and cayenne pepper. Return duck to pan and turn pieces to coat them in spice mixture. Stir in coconut milk and bring to the boil. Cover and cook over a low heat for about 40 minutes or until duck is tender. Garnish and serve hot.

Serves 4.

CHICKEN BIRYANI

625 g (1¼ lb) boneless chicken breasts (fillets),
  skinned
500 g (1 lb/3 cups) basmati rice, washed
6 tablespoons vegetable oil
6 green cardamom pods, bruised
½ teaspoon cumin seeds
2 onions, finely sliced
4 cloves garlic, crushed
5 cm (2 in) piece fresh root ginger, grated
155 ml (5 fl oz/⅔ cup) natural yogurt
salt and pepper
large pinch saffron threads
6 teaspoons boiling water
few drops red food colouring
3 tablespoons flaked almonds, toasted, and
  2 tablespoons sultanas, to garnish

Cut chicken into 2 cm (¾ in) cubes. Set
aside. Soak rice in cold water for 30
minutes, then drain. Heat 60 ml (2 fl oz/¼
cup) oil in a large heavy-based pan, add
cardamom pods and cumin seeds and fry for
1 minute. Stir in onions, garlic, ginger and
chicken and cook for about 5 minutes,
stirring, over a high heat until chicken is
browned all over. Stir in yogurt 1 tablespoon
at a time, then add 125 ml (4 fl oz/½ cup)
water. Cover and simmer for 15 minutes.

Heat remaining oil in separate pan, stir in
rice and fry for 2-3 minutes, until golden,
stirring all the time. Stir into chicken
mixture and season with salt and pepper.
Cover and simmer for 12-15 minutes, until
rice and chicken are tender. Soak saffron in
boiling water for 5 minutes. Add 6 teaspoons
water to food colouring. Pour liquids into
separate parts of rice and fork in to colour it
yellow, red and white. Serve hot, garnished
with almonds and sultanas.

Serves 4.

— GOLDEN STEAMED CHICKEN —

125 g (4 oz/¾ cup) basmati rice
1.75 kg (3½ lb) chicken
3 tablespoons vegetable oil
½ teaspoon chilli powder
60 g (2 oz/⅓ cup) raisins
60 g (2 oz/½ cup) flaked almonds
1 tablespoon chopped fresh thyme
salt and cayenne pepper
½ teaspoon ground cumin
½ teaspoon turmeric
1 teaspoon ground coriander
2 teaspoons Garam Masala, see page 11
125 ml (4 fl oz/½ cup) hot water
thyme sprigs, to garnish

Wash rice thoroughly and soak in cold water for 30 minutes, then drain. Wash chicken, pat dry with absorbent kitchen paper and set aside. Heat 1 tablespoon oil in a saucepan, add rice and fry, stirring, for 2-3 minutes, until golden brown. Stir in chilli powder, raisins, almonds, thyme, 185 ml (6 fl oz/¾ cup) water and salt. Bring to the boil, then cover and simmer for 10-12 minutes, until rice has absorbed all the liquid. Leave to cool, then use to stuff chicken.

Truss chicken, then place in a steamer and steam for 1 hour. Heat remaining oil in a large pan, add cumin, turmeric, coriander and garam masala. Season with salt and cayenne pepper and fry for 1 minute. Transfer chicken to this pan and fry for 5 minutes, turning chicken until well coated. Pour hot water down side of pan, cover and cook over a low heat for 15-20 minutes, until tender. Serve hot, garnished with thyme sprigs.

Serves 4.

— DUCK WITH HONEY & LIME —

four 250 g (8 oz) duck portions, skinned
2 tablespoons vegetable oil
1 onion, finely chopped
2 cloves garlic, crushed
2.5 cm (1 in) piece fresh root ginger, finely sliced
8 green cardamom pods, bruised
7.5 cm (3 in) cinnamon stick
3 tablespoons clear honey
juice of 2 limes
twists of lime, to garnish

Wash duck and pat dry with absorbent kitchen paper. Slash the meaty parts of the duck 2 or 3 times.

Place duck in a shallow non-metal dish and set aside. Heat oil in a frying pan, add onion and cook, stirring, until soft. Stir in garlic, ginger, cardamom pods and cinnamon and fry for 2 minutes more. Stir in honey and lime juice, then pour over duck portions. Cover and leave in a cool place for 2-3 hours to marinate.

Preheat oven to 200C (400F/Gas 6). Transfer duck to a roasting tin if shallow dish is not ovenproof, then cook for 45-60 minutes, basting occasionally with marinade, until browned and tender. Serve hot, garnished with lime twists.

Serves 4.

MURGHAL SHREDDED DUCK

500 g (1 lb) boneless duck breasts, skinned
60 ml (2 fl oz/¼ cup) vegetable oil
1 onion, finely chopped
1 quantity Cashew Nut Masala made with 125 g (4 oz/
    ¾ cup) cashew nuts, see page 10
1 teaspoon turmeric
60 g (2 oz/⅔ cup) desiccated coconut
90 g (3 oz/½ cup) sultanas
155 ml (5 fl oz/⅔ cup) natural yogurt
6 tablespoons double (thick) cream
60 g (2 oz/⅓ cup) unsalted cashew nuts
1 green chilli, seeded and chopped

Wash duck breasts and pat dry with absorbent kitchen paper.

Slice duck into 0.5 cm (¼ in) thick strips. Heat 3 tablespoons oil in a large frying pan, add duck and cook over a high heat for about 5 minutes, until browned all over. Remove duck from pan with a slotted spoon and set aside. Add onion to pan and cook, stirring, for 5 minutes or until soft. Stir in cashew nut masala and turmeric and fry for 2 minutes. Stir in coconut, sultanas, yogurt, cream and duck.

Cover and cook over a low heat for 15-20 minutes, stirring occasionally, until duck is tender. Just before serving, heat remaining oil in a small pan, add cashew nuts and fry for 2-3 minutes, until golden. Add chilli and fry for 1 minute more. Transfer duck to a warm serving dish, spoon over cashew nut and chilli mixture. Serve hot.

Serves 4-6.

CHICKEN WITH LENTILS

250 g (8 oz) boneless chicken breasts (fillets)
250 g (8 oz/1¼ cups) red split lentils
½ teaspoon turmeric
60 ml (2 fl oz/¼ cup) vegetable oil
6 green cardamom pods, bruised
1 onion, finely sliced
1 cm (½ in) piece fresh root ginger, grated
salt and cayenne pepper
6 teaspoons lemon juice
1 teaspoon cumin seeds
2 cloves garlic, finely sliced

Wash chicken, pat dry and cut into cubes.
Set aside.

Wash lentils, put in a large saucepan and
add 940 ml (30 fl oz/3¾ cups) water and
turmeric. Bring to the boil, then cover and
simmer for 20-30 minutes or until tender.
Drain thoroughly. Meanwhile, heat half the
oil in a large saucepan, add cardamom pods
and fry for 1 minute. Add onion and fry,
stirring frequently, for about 8 minutes,
until golden brown. Add chicken and fry for
5 minutes, until browned all over. Add
ginger and fry for 1 minute more. Season
with salt and cayenne pepper.

Stir in lemon juice and 155 ml (5 fl oz/⅔
cup) water and cover. Simmer for 25-30
minutes or until chicken is tender. Stir in
lentil mixture and cook, stirring, for 5
minutes. Meanwhile, heat remaining oil,
add cumin and garlic and fry, stirring, for 1-
2 minutes, until garlic is golden. Transfer
chicken and lentils to serving dish and pour
garlic mixture over. Serve hot.

Serves 4.

CHICKEN TIKKA

750 g (1½ lb) boneless chicken breasts (fillets), skinned
155 ml (5 fl oz/⅔ cup) natural yogurt
2.5 cm (1 in) piece fresh root ginger, grated
2 cloves garlic, crushed
1 teaspoon chilli powder
3 teaspoons ground coriander
salt
6 teaspoons lime juice
2 tablespoons vegetable oil
lime slices, to garnish

Wash chicken, pat dry with absorbent kitchen paper and cut into 2 cm (¾ in) cubes. Thread onto short skewers.

Put skewered chicken into a shallow non-metal dish. In a small bowl, mix together yogurt, ginger, garlic, chilli powder, coriander, salt, lime juice and oil. Pour over skewered chicken and turn to coat completely in marinade. Cover and leave in a cool place for 6 hours or overnight to allow chicken to absorb flavours.

Heat grill. Place skewered chicken on grill rack and cook for 5-7 minutes, turning skewers and basting occasionally with any remaining marinade, until cooked through. Serve hot, garnished with lime slices.

Serves 4.

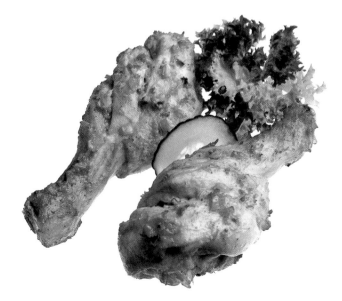

— FRIED CHICKEN DRUMSTICKS —

8 chicken drumsticks, skinned
1 onion, finely chopped
1 green chilli, seeded and finely chopped
2.5 cm (1 in) piece fresh root ginger, grated
155 ml (5 fl oz/⅔ cup) natural yogurt
¼ teaspoon chilli powder
salt and pepper
vegetable oil for deep frying
2 tablespoons chopped fresh coriander
lettuce leaves and cucumber slices, to garnish

Wash chicken drumsticks and pat dry with absorbent kitchen paper. Slash the meaty parts 2 or 3 times and place in a shallow non-metal dish.

Mix together onion, chilli, ginger, yogurt and chilli powder and season with salt and pepper. Pour over drumsticks and turn them in marinade until coated completely. Cover and leave in a cool place for 2-3 hours to allow chicken to absorb flavours.

Half-fill a deep-fat pan or fryer with oil and heat to 190C (375F) or until a cube of day-old bread browns in 40 seconds. Fry drumsticks 4 at a time for 10-12 minutes, until they are browned and cooked through. Drain on absorbent kitchen paper and keep warm while frying the rest. Sprinkle with fresh coriander and serve hot, garnished with lettuce and cucumber slices.

Serves 4.

CHICKEN IN SPICY SAUCE

8 chicken thighs, skinned
250 g (8 oz) can tomatoes, drained
6 teaspoons tomato purée (paste)
6 teaspoons chilli sauce
2 teaspoons sugar
3 teaspoons Garam Masala, see page 11
6 teaspoons light soy sauce
5 cm (2 in) piece fresh root ginger, grated
2 cloves garlic, crushed
juice of 1 lime and 1 lemon
twists of lime and lemon, to garnish

Wash chicken and pat dry with absorbent kitchen paper. Slash meaty parts 2 or 3 times. Place in a shallow non-metal dish.

Put tomatoes, tomato purée (paste), chilli sauce, sugar, garam masala, soy sauce, ginger, garlic, and lime and lemon juices in a blender or food processor fitted with a metal blade and process until smooth. Pour over chicken, cover and leave in a cool place for 2-3 hours to allow chicken to absorb flavours.

Preheat oven to 190C (375F/Gas 5). Put chicken and the sauce in a roasting tin and cook, uncovered, for 45-50 minutes, basting with sauce 2 or 3 times, until tender and cooked. Serve hot, garnished with lime and lemon twists.

Serves 4.

— CURRIED CHICKEN LIVERS —

250 g (8 oz) chicken livers
2 tablespoons vegetable oil
2 onions, finely sliced
3 cloves garlic, crushed
2 teaspoons Garam Masala, see page 11
½ teaspoon turmeric
salt and pepper
6 teaspoons lemon juice
2 tablespoons chopped fresh parsley
parsley sprigs, to garnish

Wash chicken livers and remove any green tinged parts. Set aside.

Heat oil in a frying pan, add onions and cook over a medium heat, stirring, for about 8 minutes, until soft and golden brown. Stir in garlic, garam masala and turmeric and season with salt and pepper.

Fry for 1 minute, then stir in chicken livers and fry for about 5 minutes, stirring frequently, until livers are browned on outsides but still slightly pink in the centres. Sprinkle with lemon juice and parsley. Serve hot, garnished with sprigs of parsley.

Serves 4 as a starter.

Note: Frozen chicken livers can be used: thaw at room temperature for 3-4 hours before using.

SWEET SAFFRON RICE

250 g (8 oz/1½ cups) basmati rice
1 teaspoon saffron threads
3 tablespoons boiling water
3 tablespoons vegetable oil
6 cloves
6 green cardamom pods, bruised
7.5 cm (3 in) cinnamon stick
90 g (3 oz/½ cup) raisins
3 tablespoons sugar
salt
parsley sprigs, to garnish

Place rice in a sieve and wash under cold running water until water runs clear.

Put rice in a bowl with 625 ml (20 fl oz/2½ cups) water and soak for 30 minutes. Put saffron in a small bowl, add boiling water and leave to soak for 5 minutes. Heat oil in a heavy-based saucepan, add cloves, carda-mom pods and cinnamon and fry for 1 minute. Drain rice and reserve the soaking water. Add rice to the pan and fry for 2-3 minutes, until opaque and light golden.

Stir in reserved water, saffron and its soaking water, raisins and sugar and season with salt. Bring to the boil, then lower the heat and simmer, covered, for 12-15 minutes, stirring once or twice, until liquid is absorbed and rice is very tender. Serve hot, garnished with parsley.

Serves 4.

Note: The whole spices in the rice are not meant to be eaten.

FRAGRANT FRIED RICE

185 g (6 oz/1¼ cups) basmati rice
3 tablespoons vegetable oil
8 cloves
4 black cardamom pods, bruised
1 bay leaf
7.5 cm (3 in) cinnamon stick
1 teaspoon black peppercorns
1 teaspoon cumin seeds
1 teaspoon coriander seeds
1 onion, sliced into rings
1 small cauliflower, cut into tiny flowerets
salt
onion rings and bay leaves, to garnish

Place rice in a sieve and wash under cold running water until water runs clear. Put in a bowl with 625 ml (20 fl oz/2½ cups) water and soak for 30 minutes. Heat oil in a heavy-based saucepan, add cloves, cardamom pods, bay leaf, cinnamon, peppercorns and cumin and coriander seeds and fry for 1 minute. Add onion and cook for 5 minutes, until softened. Drain rice and reserve the soaking water.

Add rice to the pan and fry for 2-3 minutes, until opaque and light golden. Stir in reserved water and cauliflower and season with salt. Bring to the boil, lower heat and simmer, covered, for 12-15 minutes, stirring once or twice, until liquid is absorbed and rice and cauliflower are tender. Serve hot, garnished with onion rings and bay leaves.

Serves 4.

Note: Do not eat the whole spices.

LENTIL-STUFFED PEPPERS

125 g (4 oz/⅔ cup) red split lentils
60 ml (2 fl oz/¼ cup) vegetable oil
4 green or red peppers (capsicums)
1 teaspoon cumin seeds
2 onions, finely chopped
2 green chillies, seeded and chopped
2.5 cm (1 in) piece fresh root ginger, grated
3 teaspoons ground coriander
salt and pepper
2 tablespoons chopped fresh coriander
coriander leaves, to garnish

Wash lentils, then soak in cold water for 30 minutes.

Heat half the oil in a frying pan and fry peppers (capsicums) for 3-5 minutes, until golden brown on all sides. Drain on absorbent kitchen paper and leave to cool. Add remaining oil to pan, then add cumin seeds and fry until just beginning to pop. Add onions and chillies and fry, stirring, for 8 minutes, until onions are soft and golden brown. Stir in ginger and ground coriander. Drain lentils and add to pan with 315 ml (10 fl oz/1¼ cups) water and stir well.

Cook, covered, over low heat for 15-20 minutes, until tender and liquid has been absorbed. Season with salt and pepper and add fresh coriander. Preheat oven to 180C (350F/Gas 4). Cut tops from peppers (capsicums) and remove seeds. Stuff peppers (capsicums) with lentil mixture and replace tops. Stand in an ovenproof dish and cook for 15-20 minutes, until soft. Serve hot, garnished with coriander leaves.

Serves 4.

STUFFED OKRA

500 g (1 lb) small okra
6 teaspoons mango powder
3 teaspoons ground coriander
2 teaspoons ground cumin
¼ teaspoon cayenne pepper
1 teaspoon Garam Masala, see page 11
salt
2 tablespoons vegetable oil
1 onion, sliced
6 tomatoes, skinned
lemon slices, to garnish

Wash okra and pat dry with absorbent kitchen paper.

Trim off okra stems, then cut a slit along one side of each pod, stopping 0.5 cm (¼ in) from each end. Mix mango powder, coriander, cumin, cayenne pepper, garam masala and salt to taste together. Prise open okra pods with your thumb and sprinkle a little of the spice mixture inside each pod. Set aside.

Heat oil in a large saucepan and add onion. Fry for about 5 minutes, until softened. Cut tomatoes into wedges and remove seeds and discard. Add tomatoes to pan and cook, stirring once or twice, for 2 minutes. Add okra and cook gently, covered, for 10-15 minutes, stirring occasionally, until okra are tender. Serve hot, garnished with lemon.

Serves 4.

Note: Mango powder, often called amchoor powder, is available from Asian shops.

— DHAL BALLS WITH YOGURT —

125 g (4 oz/²/₃ cup) whole green lentils
440 ml (14 fl oz/1¾ cups) natural yogurt
6 tablespoons chopped fresh coriander
¼ teaspoon chilli powder
4 tablespoons shredded fresh coconut
60 g (2 oz/1 cup) fresh breadcrumbs
2 fresh green chillies, seeded and chopped
2.5 cm (1 in) piece fresh root ginger, grated
1 egg, beaten
salt and pepper
60 g (2 oz/½ cup) wholewheat flour
vegetable oil for deep frying
coriander leaves, to garnish

Put lentils in a sieve and wash thoroughly.

Pick over lentils and remove any grit. Put in a bowl, cover with cold water and soak for 2 hours. Meanwhile, mix yogurt with 2 tablespoons coriander, and chilli powder. Cover and chill. Drain lentils, cover with fresh water and simmer for 30 minutes or until tender. Purée in a blender or food processor or mash well. Transfer to a bowl, add 2 tablespoons coconut, breadcrumbs, remaining coriander, chillies, ginger and egg. Season with salt and pepper and mix well. Chill for 30 minutes.

With damp hands, carefully roll mixture into 2.5 cm (1 in) balls, then roll balls in flour to coat completely. Half-fill a deep-fat pan or fryer with oil and heat to 190C (375F) or until a cube of day-old bread browns in 40 seconds. Fry about 6 balls at a time for 2-3 minutes, until golden. Drain well. Serve hot with yogurt sauce, sprinkled with remaining coconut and garnished with coriander leaves.

Serves 4.

— CARROTS WITH FRESH DILL —

500 g (1 lb) carrots
1 tablespoon vegetable oil
30 g (1 oz/6 teaspoons) butter or ghee
¾ teaspoon cumin seeds
pinch ground asafoetida
1 cm (½ in) piece fresh root ginger, finely chopped
2 fresh green chillies, seeded and finely sliced
1 teaspoon ground coriander
¼ teaspoon turmeric
4 tablespoons chopped fresh dill
salt
dill sprigs, to garnish

Cut carrots into 0.3 x 2.5 cm (⅛ x 1 in) sticks and set aside.

Heat oil and butter or ghee in a heavy-based pan and fry cumin seeds for about 30 seconds, until they begin to pop. Add asafoetida, ginger, chillies, coriander and turmeric and fry for 2 minutes. Stir in carrots and 6 tablespoons water.

Cook over a medium heat, covered, for 5 minutes or until carrots are just tender. Uncover, add chopped dill, season with salt and cook over a high heat for about 2 minutes to evaporate any excess liquid. Serve hot, garnished with dill sprigs.

Serves 4.

Note: This recipe is also delicious, chilled and served as a salad.

— MIXED VEGETABLE CURRY —

3 tablespoons vegetable oil
1 onion, sliced
1 teaspoon ground cumin
1 teaspoon chilli powder
2 teaspoons ground coriander
1 teaspoon turmeric
250 g (8 oz) potatoes, diced
185 g (6 oz) cauliflower flowerets
125 g (4 oz) green beans, sliced
185 g (6 oz) carrots, diced
4 tomatoes, skinned and chopped
315 ml (10 fl oz/1¼ cups) hot vegetable stock
onion rings, to garnish

Heat oil in a large saucepan, add onion and fry for 5 minutes, until softened. Stir in cumin, chilli powder, coriander and turmeric and cook for 2 minutes, stirring occasionally. Add potatoes, cauliflower, green beans and carrots, tossing them in the spices until coated.

Add tomatoes and stock and cover. Bring to the boil, then reduce heat and simmer for 10-12 minutes or until vegetables are just tender. Serve hot, garnished with onion rings.

Serves 4.

Variation: Use any mixture of vegetables to make a total of 750 g (1½ lb) – turnips, swedes, courgettes (zucchini), aubergines (eggplant), parsnips and leeks are all suitable for this curry.

SPICED BROWN LENTILS

250 g (8 oz/1¼ cups) whole brown lentils
315 ml (10 fl oz/1¼ cups) Coconut Milk, see page 11
¼ teaspoon chilli powder
½ teaspoon turmeric
2 tablespoons vegetable oil
1 onion, finely chopped
4 curry leaves
½ stick lemon grass
7.5 cm (3 in) cinnamon stick
sprigs of lemon thyme, to garnish

Wash lentils, put in a bowl, cover with cold water and leave to soak for 6 hours or overnight.

Drain lentils and put them in a large saucepan with coconut milk, chilli powder and turmeric. Bring to the boil, then simmer, covered, for 30 minutes or until just tender. Heat oil in a separate pan, add onion, curry leaves, lemon grass and cinnamon and fry over a medium heat, stirring, for 8 minutes or until onion is soft and golden brown.

Stir into lentil mixture and simmer for a further 10 minutes or until liquid has evaporated and lentils are soft but not broken up. Remove whole spices and serve hot, garnished with thyme sprigs.

Serves 4.

Note: Substitute a few sprigs of lemon thyme if lemon grass is unavailable. Look for lemon grass at Asian and Oriental shops and the larger supermarkets.

CURRIED CHICK-PEAS

185 g (6 oz/1 cup) dried chick-peas
2 tablespoons vegetable oil
1 small onion, finely chopped
2.5 cm (1 in) piece fresh root ginger, grated
2 cloves garlic, crushed
½ teaspoon turmeric
1 teaspoon ground cumin
1 teaspoon Garam Masala, see page 11
½ teaspoon chilli powder
salt
2 tablespoons chopped fresh coriander

Wash chick-peas well, then put them in a bowl, cover with cold water and leave to soak overnight.

Drain chick-peas, then put in a saucepan with 500 ml (16 fl oz/2 cups) fresh cold water. Bring to the boil for 10 minutes, then reduce heat and simmer, partially covered, for 1 hour. In a separate pan, heat oil, add onion and fry for about 8 minutes, until soft and golden brown.

Add ginger, garlic, turmeric, cumin, garam masala and chilli powder and fry for 1 minute. Stir in chick-peas and their cooking water and season with salt. Bring to the boil, then simmer, covered, for 20 minutes, until chick-peas are very tender but still whole. Serve hot, sprinkled with chopped fresh coriander.

Serves 4.

— MUNG BEANSPROUT SALAD —

185 g (6 oz/1 cup) mung beans
2 green chillies, seeded and chopped
2.5 cm (1 in) piece fresh root ginger, grated
30 g (1 oz/⅔ cup) fresh coconut, shredded
½ cucumber, diced
juice of 1 lemon
salt and pepper
1 mango
2 tablespoons vegetable oil
½ teaspoon mustard seeds
coriander leaves and shreds of lemon peel, to garnish,
  if desired

Wash beans, put in a bowl and cover with cold water.

Soak beans in the water for 30 minutes. Drain, then place in a sprouting tray or wrap in a damp tea-towel and leave for about 2 days, rinsing thoroughly every 12 hours, until the beans germinate. Rinse well and drain. Place sprouts in a bowl and stir in chillies, ginger, coconut, cucumber and lemon juice. Season with salt and pepper.

Peel and stone mango, then dice flesh and stir into salad. Heat oil in a small pan and add mustard seeds and fry for 1 minute, until they begin to pop. Pour contents of pan over the salad and toss well to combine. Chill for at least 30 minutes. Serve garnished with coriander leaves and lemon peel, if desired.

Serves 4-6.

Variations: Try sprouting chick-peas, whole wheat, aduki beans or alfalfa seeds for this salad.

TAMIL NADU VEGETABLES

125 g (4 oz/²⁄₃ cup) red split lentils
½ teaspoon turmeric
1 small aubergine (eggplant)
60 ml (2 fl oz/¼ cup) vegetable oil
30 g (1 oz/⅓ cup) desiccated coconut
1 teaspoon cumin seeds
½ teaspoon mustard seeds
2 dried red chillies, crushed
1 red pepper (capsicum), seeded and sliced
125 g (4 oz) courgettes (zucchini), thickly sliced
90 g (3 oz) green beans, cut into 2 cm (¾ in) pieces
155 ml (5 fl oz/²⁄₃ cup) vegetable stock
salt
red pepper (capsicum) strips, to garnish

Wash lentils and put in a large saucepan with turmeric and 625 ml (20 fl oz/2½ cups) water. Bring to the boil, then reduce heat and simmer, covered, for 15-20 minutes, until lentils are soft. Meanwhile, cut aubergine (eggplant) into 1 cm (½ in) dice. Heat oil in a large shallow pan, add coconut, cumin and mustard seeds and chillies.

Fry for 1 minute, then add aubergine (eggplant), red pepper (capsicum), courgettes (zucchini), green beans, stock and salt. Bring to the boil, then simmer, covered, for 10-15 minutes, until the vegetables are just tender. Stir in lentils and any cooking liquid and cook for a further 5 minutes. Serve hot, garnished with red pepper (capsicum) strips.

Serves 4.

SPINACH & BEAN DUMPLINGS

185 g (6 oz/1 cup) yellow split mung beans
60 g (2 oz) frozen chopped spinach, thawed
2 tablespoons chopped fresh coriander
2 fresh green chillies, seeded and chopped
large pinch baking powder
½ teaspoon salt
vegetable oil for deep frying
chilli flowers, to garnish

Put beans in a bowl, cover them with water and leave to soak for 4 hours. Drain and rinse under cold running water.

Put beans in a blender or food processor fitted with a metal blade and process until smooth, light and fluffy, scraping mixture from sides of bowl several times. Press excess water from spinach and mix into the ground beans. Stir in coriander, chillies, baking powder and salt.

Half-fill a deep-fat pan or fryer with oil and heat to 190C (375F) or until a cube of day-old bread browns in 40 seconds. Drop 6 heaped teaspoonfuls of mixture into the hot oil and fry for 4-5 minutes or until golden brown. Drain dumplings on absorbent kitchen paper and keep warm while frying remainder. Serve hot, garnished with chilli flowers.

Serves 4.

MUSHROOM CURRY

500 g (1 lb) button mushrooms
2 fresh green chillies, seeded
2 teaspoons ground coriander
1 teaspoon ground cumin
½ teaspoon chilli powder
2 cloves garlic, crushed
1 onion, cut into wedges
155 ml (5 fl oz/⅔ cup) Coconut Milk, see page 11
salt
30 g (1 oz/6 teaspoons) butter or ghee
bay leaves, to garnish

Wipe mushrooms and trim stalks, then set aside.

Put chillies, ground coriander, cumin, chilli powder, garlic, onion, coconut milk and salt to taste in a blender or food processor fitted with a metal blade and blend until smooth.

Melt butter in a saucepan, add mushrooms and fry for 3-4 minutes, until golden brown. Pour over spicy coconut milk and simmer, uncovered, for 10 minutes or until mushrooms are tender. Serve hot, garnished with bay leaves.

Serves 4.

PEPPERS WITH CAULIFLOWER

60 ml (2 fl oz/¼ cup) vegetable oil
1 large onion, sliced
2 cloves garlic, crushed
2 green chillies, seeded and chopped
1 cauliflower, cut into small flowerets
½ teaspoon turmeric
1 teaspoon Garam Masala, see page 11
1 green pepper (capsicum)
1 red pepper (capsicum)
1 orange or yellow pepper (capsicum)
salt and pepper
1 tablespoon chopped fresh coriander, to garnish

Heat oil in a large saucepan, add onion and fry over a medium heat for 8 minutes or until soft and golden brown. Stir in garlic, chillies and cauliflower and fry for 5 minutes, stirring occasionally. Stir in turmeric and garam masala and fry for 1 minute.

Reduce heat, add 60 ml (2 fl oz/¼ cup) water and cook, covered, for 10-15 minutes, until cauliflower is almost tender. Cut peppers (capsicums) in half lengthwise, remove stalks and seeds, then slice peppers (capsicums) finely. Add to pan and cook for a further 3-5 minutes, until softened. Season with salt and pepper. Serve hot, garnished with chopped coriander.

Serves 4.

— CHEESY STUFFED TOMATOES —

8 tomatoes
2 tablespoons vegetable oil
1 small onion, finely chopped
1 clove garlic, crushed
2.5 cm (1 in) piece fresh root ginger, grated
1 teaspoon ground cumin
½ teaspoon turmeric
½ teaspoon cayenne pepper
2 teaspoons ground coriander
salt
125 g (4 oz/½ cup) fresh Indian cheese or natural
    fromage frais
30 g (1 oz/¼ cup) Cheddar cheese, grated
1 tablespoon chopped fresh coriander

Cut a slice from the top of each tomato. Scoop out centres and discard seeds, then chop pulp and reserve. Turn tomatoes upside down on absorbent kitchen paper and leave to drain. Heat oil in a small frying pan, add onion and fry for 5 minutes, stirring occasionally, until soft. Stir in garlic and ginger and fry for 1 minute. Stir in cumin, turmeric, cayenne pepper and ground coriander. Season with salt and fry for 1 minute more.

Stir in tomato pulp and cook, uncovered, for about 5 minutes, until thick. Preheat oven to 190C (375F/Gas 5). Stir fresh cheese or fromage frais and half the Cheddar into spice mixture and spoon into tomato shells. Sprinkle remaining Cheddar over the tops and place on a baking tray. Cook for 10-15 minutes, until tops are golden brown and tomatoes soft. Sprinkle with chopped coriander and serve hot.

Serves 4.

ONION BHAJIS

90 g (3 oz/¾ cup) chick-pea flour, sifted
1 tablespoon vegetable oil plus extra for deep frying
1 teaspoon ground coriander
1 teaspoon ground cumin
2 fresh green chillies, seeded and finely chopped
125 ml (4 fl oz/½ cup) warm water
salt
2 onions, finely sliced
herb sprigs, to garnish

Put flour in blender or food processor fitted with a metal blade.

Add oil, coriander, cumin, chillies and water. Season with salt. Process until well blended and smooth, then pour batter into a bowl. Cover and leave in a warm place for 30 minutes. Stir in onions.

Half-fill a deep-fat pan or fryer with oil and heat to 190C (375F) or until a cube of day-old bread browns in 40 seconds. Drop about five 2 tablespoon amounts into the oil and fry for 5-6 minutes, until golden. Drain on absorbent kitchen paper. Serve hot, garnished with sprigs of herbs.

Serves 4.

Note: Make sure that the oil doesn't become too hot: the bhajis must fry slowly so the centres cook through.

SPICY OKRA

375 g (12 oz) okra
2 tablespoons vegetable oil
2.5 cm (1 in) piece fresh root ginger, grated
1 teaspoon turmeric
½ teaspoon chilli powder
1 teaspoon chick-pea flour
salt
315 ml (10 fl oz/1¼ cups) natural yogurt
2 tablespoons chopped fresh coriander, to garnish

Wash okra and pat dry with absorbent kitchen paper, then cut into thick slices.

Heat oil in a saucepan, add okra and fry, stirring occasionally, for 4 minutes. Stir in ginger, turmeric, chilli powder and flour. Season with salt and fry for 1 minute more.

Stir in 3 tablespoons water, then cover and cook gently for 10 minutes or until okra is tender. Stir in yogurt and reheat gently. Serve hot, sprinkled with coriander.

Serves 4.

Note: Choose okra pods that are about 10 cm (4 in) long – larger pods are tough and stringy to eat.

DRY POTATO CURRY

500 g (1 lb) waxy potatoes
salt
2 tablespoons vegetable oil
1 teaspoon mustard seeds
1 onion, finely sliced
2 cloves garlic, crushed
2.5 cm (1 in) piece fresh root ginger, grated
1 fresh green chilli, seeded and chopped
1 teaspoon turmeric
½ teaspoon cayenne pepper
1 teaspoon ground cumin
green pepper (capsicum) strips, to garnish, if desired

Cut potatoes into 2 cm (¾ in) chunks.

Cook potatoes in boiling salted water for 6-8 minutes, until just tender, then drain and set aside. Heat oil in a large saucepan, add mustard seeds and fry for 30 seconds or until they begin to pop. Add onion and fry for 5 minutes, until soft but not brown. Stir in garlic and ginger and fry for 1 minute more.

Add potatoes, chilli, turmeric, cayenne and cumin and stir well. Cook, covered, for 3-5 minutes, stirring occasionally, until potatoes are very tender and coated with spices. Serve hot, garnished with green pepper (capsicum) strips, if desired.

Serves 4.

FISH IN A PACKET

four 185-250 g (6-8 oz) fish steaks, such as sea bass,
   cod or salmon
1-2 fresh or frozen banana leaves, optional
salt and pepper
60 g (2 oz/1¼ cups) finely grated fresh coconut
60 g (2 oz) fresh mint, chopped
4 cloves garlic, crushed
1 teaspoon ground cumin
4 fresh green chillies, seeded and chopped
6 teaspoons lemon juice
60 ml (2 fl oz/¼ cup) cider vinegar
1 tablespoon vegetable oil
8 dried curry leaves, optional
mint leaves and lemon slices, to garnish

Wipe fish steaks and place each in centre of
a 30 cm (12 in) square of banana leaf, if
using, or foil. Sprinkle fish with salt and
pepper. Mix together coconut, mint, garlic,
cumin, chillies and lemon juice. Spoon a
quarter of mixture over each fish steak. Fold
sides of banana leaf or foil over to seal
completely. Tie banana leaf parcels with
fine string, if necessary.

Pour vinegar, oil and 185 ml (6 fl oz/¾ cup)
water into base of a large steamer, add curry
leaves and bring to the boil. Steam parcels
for 12-15 minutes or until fish flakes easily.
Open parcels and serve, garnished with mint
and lemon slices.

Serves 4.

— HOT MUSSELS WITH CUMIN —

1.5 kg (3 lb) mussels
2 tablespoons vegetable oil
1 large onion, finely chopped
2.5 cm (1 in) piece fresh root ginger, grated
6 cloves garlic, crushed
2 fresh green chillies, seeded and finely chopped
½ teaspoon turmeric
2 teaspoons ground cumin
90 g (3 oz/1¾ cups) shredded fresh coconut
2 tablespoons chopped fresh coriander
coriander sprigs, to garnish

Scrub mussels clean in several changes of fresh cold water and pull off beards.

Discard any mussels that are cracked or do not close tightly when tapped. Set aside. Heat oil in a large saucepan and add onion. Fry, stirring, for 5 minutes, until soft, then add ginger, garlic, chillies, turmeric and cumin. Fry 2 minutes, stirring constantly.

Add mussels, coconut and 250 ml (8 fl oz/1 cup) water and bring to the boil. Cover and cook over a high heat, shaking pan frequently, for about 5 minutes or until almost all the shells have opened. Discard any that do not open. Spoon mussels into a serving dish, pour over cooking liquid and sprinkle with chopped coriander. Garnish with coriander sprigs and serve at once.

Serves 4.

CORIANDER & CHILLI FISH

875 g (1¾ lb) white fish fillets, such as monkfish,
    sole or plaice
4 teaspoons lemon juice
salt and pepper
90 g (3 oz) fresh coriander leaves
4 fresh green chillies, seeded and chopped
3 cloves garlic, crushed
250 ml (8 fl oz/1 cup) natural yogurt
vegetable oil for deep frying
lemon wedges and coriander leaves, to garnish

Trim any skin and bones from fish, then cut
flesh into 2.5 x 7.5 cm (1 x 3 in) strips.

Spread fish strips in a shallow non-metal
dish and sprinkle with lemon juice and salt
and pepper. Set aside in a cool place. Put
coriander, chillies, garlic and 1-2 tablespoons water in a blender or food processor
fitted with a metal blade and process until
smooth, frequently scraping mixture down
from sides. Squeeze out excess liquid from
paste, place in a shallow dish and stir in
yogurt.

Heat oil in a deep-fat pan or fryer to 180C
(350F) or until a cube of day-old bread
browns in 35 seconds. Drain fish and pat dry
with absorbent kitchen paper. Dip the strips
in yogurt mixture, coating them all over and
fry a few at a time for 2-3 minutes, until
golden brown. Drain on absorbent kitchen
paper, then serve at once, garnished with
lemon wedges and coriander leaves.

Serves 4.

SOLE WITH DILL STUFFING

four 185 g (6 oz) sole fillets, skinned
3 teaspoons lemon juice
salt and pepper
2 tablespoons vegetable oil
1 clove garlic, crushed
2.5 cm (1 in) piece fresh root ginger, grated
¼ teaspoon cayenne pepper
¼ teaspoon turmeric
4 spring onions, finely chopped
8 tablespoons finely chopped fresh dill
dill sprigs, to garnish

Wash fish fillets and pat dry with absorbent kitchen paper.

Lay fillets skinned-side up on a work surface and sprinkle with lemon juice and salt and pepper, then set aside. Preheat oven to 180C (350F/Gas 4). Heat 1½ tablespoons oil in a frying pan. Add garlic, ginger, cayenne, turmeric and spring onions and cook over a low heat for 3 minutes or until onions are soft and golden, stirring occasionally. Remove from heat and set aside to cool, then stir in dill.

Divide stuffing between fillets and spread evenly over skinned side of fish. Roll fillets up from thickest end. Grease a shallow ovenproof dish with remaining oil and arrange sole rolls, seam-side down, in the dish with 60 ml (2 fl oz/¼ cup) water. Cover with foil and cook for 15-20 minutes or until fish flakes easily. Serve hot, with cooking juices spooned over and garnished with sprigs of dill.

Serves 4.

SPICE & GARLIC FISH FRY

750 g (1½ lb) mixed white fish fillets, such as sole,
    plaice, whiting, cod or monkfish
1 teaspoon ground cumin
½ teaspoon ground coriander
1 teaspoon ground aniseed
½ teaspoon chilli powder
3 cloves garlic, crushed
3 teaspoons lemon juice
salt
vegetable oil for deep frying
lettuce leaves and lemon slices, to garnish

Remove any skin and bones from fish, wash
and pat dry with absorbent kitchen paper.
Cut into large chunks.

Mix cumin, coriander, aniseed, chilli powder, garlic, lemon juice and salt together,
blending to a smooth paste. Spread over
fish, cover and leave in a cool place for 1
hour.

Half-fill a deep-fat pan or fryer with oil and
heat to 180C (350F) or until a cube of day-
old bread browns in 35 seconds. Cook fish, a
few pieces at a time, for 2-3 minutes, until
golden brown. Drain on absorbent kitchen
paper. Serve hot, garnished with lettuce and
lemon slices.

Serves 4.

SPICY PRAWN PATTIES

375 g (12 oz) white fish fillets, such as sole, plaice,
  cod or whiting
185 g (6 oz) peeled cooked prawns, chopped
4 spring onions, chopped
2.5 cm (1 in) piece fresh root ginger, grated
2 tablespoons chopped fresh coriander
1 tablespoon chopped fresh mint
125 g (4 oz/2 cups) fresh white breadcrumbs
salt and cayenne pepper
1 egg yolk, beaten
6 teaspoons lemon juice
90 g (3 oz/¾ cup) chick-pea flour
3 teaspoons ground coriander
60 ml (2 fl oz/¼ cup) vegetable oil for frying
mint sprigs and lemon slices, to garnish

Remove any skin and bones from fish, wash
and pat dry with absorbent kitchen paper.
Mince fish, then transfer to a bowl. Stir in
prawns, spring onions, ginger, fresh coriander, mint, 60 g (2 oz/1 cup) breadcrumbs
and salt and pepper. Add egg yolk and
lemon juice and mix well. Divide mixture
into 16 pieces and form each into 1 cm (½
in) thick round. Roll patties in remaining
breadcrumbs to coat completely.

Put flour and ground coriander in a small
bowl, season with salt and cayenne pepper,
then add 125 ml (4 fl oz/½ cup) water and
mix to a smooth batter. Heat oil in a frying
pan. Dip prawn patties in batter, then fry for
2-3 minutes on each side until golden
brown. Drain on absorbent kitchen paper
and serve hot, garnished with mint and
lemon slices.

Serves 4.

FISH IN HOT SAUCE

four 250 g (8 oz) whole fish, such as mackerel, trout,
  grey mullet or blue fish, cleaned
4 dill sprigs
4 lime slices
60 ml (2 fl oz/¼ cup) vegetable oil
4 spring onions, sliced
1 cm (½ in) piece fresh root ginger, grated
1 clove garlic, crushed
1 teaspoon mustard seeds
¼ teaspoon cayenne pepper
3 teaspoons tamarind paste
6 teaspoons tomato purée (paste)
dill sprigs and lime slices, to garnish

Wash fish and pat dry with absorbent
kitchen paper. Slash 2 or 3 times on each
side, tuck a sprig of dill and a lime slice
inside each fish, then set aside. Heat 2
tablespoons of oil in a small pan. Add
onions and cook, stirring, for 2-3 minutes,
until softened. Add ginger, garlic and mustard seeds and fry for 1 minute more, until
mustard seeds start to pop.

Stir in cayenne pepper, tamarind paste,
tomato purée (paste) and 90 ml (3 fl oz/⅓
cup) water. Bring to the boil and simmer,
uncovered, for about 5 minutes, until thickened slightly. Meanwhile, heat grill. Place
fish on grill rack, brush with remaining oil
and cook for about 5 minutes on each side,
basting occasionally with oil, until flesh
flakes easily. Serve hot with the sauce,
garnished with dill and lime slices.

Serves 4.

– STEAMED FISH & VEGETABLES –

four 250 g (8 oz) whole red mullet, red snapper or sea
   bream, cleaned
4 teaspoons Garam Masala, see page 11
½ teaspoon turmeric
2 tablespoons chopped fresh coriander
1 tablespoon chopped fresh parsley
2.5 cm (1 in) piece fresh root ginger, grated
4 lemon slices
2 tablespoons vegetable oil
8 new potatoes, sliced
3 carrots, sliced
4 courgettes (zucchini), sliced
salt and pepper
coriander leaves, to garnish

Wash fish and pat dry with absorbent
kitchen paper, then slash 3 times on each
side. Mix garam masala, turmeric, coriander, parsley and ginger together and rub into
flesh and skin of fish. Tuck a slice of lemon
inside each fish and set aside. Heat oil in a
frying pan, add potatoes and carrots and fry,
stirring frequently, for 5-6 minutes, until
slightly softened and beginning to brown.

Add courgettes (zucchini) to pan and fry for
1 minute more. Season with salt and pepper.
Using a slotted spoon, transfer vegetables to
a steamer. Lay fish on top, cover and steam
for 20-25 minutes or until fish flakes easily
and vegetables are tender. Serve at once,
garnished with coriander.

Serves 4.

PRAWNS & MUSTARD SEEDS

500 g (1 lb) raw Mediterranean (king) prawns
3 teaspoons mixed black and yellow mustard seeds
½ teaspoon turmeric
½ teaspoon cayenne pepper
salt
30 g (1 oz/6 teaspoons) butter or ghee, melted
strips of orange and lime peel, to garnish

Peel prawns, leaving tail shells on, then make a small incision along the spines and remove black vein. Push 2 or 3 prawns at a time onto short wooden skewers, then set aside.

Reserve 1 teaspoon mustard seeds, and grind remainder in a mortar and pestle or coffee grinder. Transfer to a small bowl and mix in turmeric and cayenne and season with salt. Add 90 ml (3 fl oz/⅓ cup) water and blend until smooth. Add prawns, turning to coat them in the marinade and leave in a cool place for 30 minutes to marinate.

Heat grill. Drain skewered prawns and place on a grill rack, brush with butter and sprinkle with reserved mustard seeds. Cook for 3-5 minutes, turning over once and basting occasionally with any remaining marinade, until prawns are just tender. Serve hot, garnished with orange and lime peel.

Serves 4.

— MADRAS CURRIED CRABS —

4 medium cooked crabs
3 tablespoons vegetable oil
1 onion, finely chopped
3 cloves garlic, finely sliced
2.5 cm (1 in) piece fresh root ginger, grated
1 beef tomato, skinned and chopped
3 fresh green chillies, seeded and chopped
2 tablespoons desiccated coconut, toasted
1 quantity Almond Masala, see page 10
250 ml (8 fl oz/1 cup) Coconut Milk, see page 11

Remove large claws from crabs and crack to make eating easier. Twist off small claws.

Pull out body sections from shells, remove finger-shaped gills and discard. Cut body sections in half with a large sharp knife or cleaver and use a skewer to remove all the white meat. Remove the greyish white stomach sac behind each head and any green coloured matter and discard. Scrape out creamy brown meat from shells and add to white meat. Use a heavy weight to tap round underside of shells and break round natural dark line, discarding the broken bits of shell. Wash main shells and set aside.

Heat oil in a large frying pan, add onion and fry, stirring frequently, for about 8 minutes or until soft and golden. Add garlic and ginger and fry for 1 minute. Stir in tomato, chillies, coconut, almond masala, coconut milk and reserved crab meat. Add crab claws and simmer, covered, for 6-8 minutes, until heated through. Spoon the mixture into crab shells and serve hot.

Serves 4.

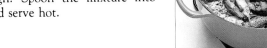

PRAWN & FISH BALL CURRY

500 g (1 lb) white fish fillets, such as sole, plaice, cod,
   whiting or monkfish, skinned
125 g (4 oz) peeled cooked prawns
90 g (3 oz/1½ cups) fresh white breadcrumbs
2 eggs, beaten separately
2 tablespoons chopped fresh coriander
2 teaspoons lemon juice
salt and pepper
2 tablespoons vegetable oil plus extra for frying
1 large onion, finely chopped
2 fresh green chillies, seeded and chopped
4 cloves garlic, crushed
½ teaspoon turmeric
155 ml (5 fl oz/⅔ cup) Coconut Milk, see page 11
440 g (14 oz) can chopped tomatoes

Wash fish and remove any bones. Mince fish
and prawns, then transfer to a large bowl.
Stir in 60 g (2 oz/1 cup) breadcrumbs, 1 egg,
coriander and lemon juice and season with
salt and pepper. Mix well and form into 24
balls. Roll balls in remaining egg, then in
remaining breadcrumbs to coat completely.
Chill for 30 minutes. Meanwhile, heat 2
tablespoons oil in a heavy-based pan, add
onion and cook, stirring, for 5 minutes until
soft.

Add chillies, garlic and turmeric and fry for
2 minutes more. Stir in coconut milk and
tomatoes and cook, uncovered, for 20
minutes, stirring occasionally, until thickened. Half-fill a deep-fat pan or fryer with
oil and heat to 190C (375F) or until a cube
of day-old bread browns in 40 seconds. Fry
fish balls for 3-5 minutes, until golden.
Drain well and serve with the sauce.

Serves 4.

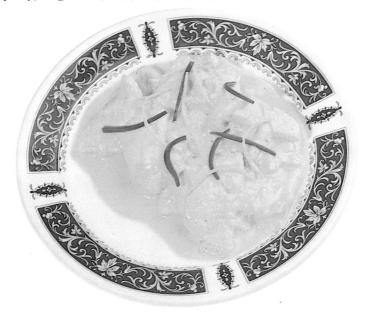

CREAMY SAFFRON FISH CURRY

750 g (1½ lb) white fish fillets, such as sole, plaice,
    whiting or cod
pinch saffron threads
2 tablespoons boiling water
3 tablespoons vegetable oil
2 onions, chopped
3 cloves garlic, crushed
2.5 cm (1 in) piece fresh root ginger, grated
1 teaspoon turmeric
3 teaspoons ground coriander
2 teaspoons Garam Masala, see page 11
salt and cayenne pepper
2 teaspoons chick-pea flour
250 ml (8 fl oz/1 cup) natural yogurt
60 ml (2 fl oz/¼ cup) double (thick) cream
lemon peel and red pepper (capsicum), to garnish

Wash fish, remove any skin and bones and
pat dry with absorbent paper. Cut into large
chunks and set aside. Put saffron in a small
bowl with water and leave to soak for about
5 minutes. Heat oil in a large shallow pan,
add onions and cook, stirring, for about 5
minutes, until soft but not coloured.

Add garlic, ginger, turmeric, coriander,
garam masala and salt and pepper and fry for
1 minute more. Stir in flour and cook for 1
minute, then remove from heat. Stir in
yogurt and cream, then return to heat and
slowly bring to the boil. Add fish, saffron
and soaking water and simmer gently, covered, for 10-15 minutes, until fish is tender
and flakes easily. Serve the fish hot, garnished with shreds of lemon peel and red
pepper (capsicum).

Serves 4.

CORIANDER FISH KEBABS

750 g (1½ lb) monkfish fillets
155 ml (5 fl oz/⅔ cup) natural yogurt
3 cloves garlic, crushed
2 teaspoons Garam Masala, see page 11
3 teaspoons ground coriander
salt and pepper
1 green chilli, seeded and cut into thin rings
1 spring onion, finely sliced
¼ lime, finely sliced

Remove any bones from fish, wash and pat dry with absorbent kitchen paper. Cut into 2.5 cm (1 in) cubes and thread onto skewers.

Mix together yogurt, garlic, garam masala and coriander and season with salt and pepper. Put kebabs in a non-metal dish and pour over yogurt marinade. Cover and leave in cool place for 2-3 hours to allow fish to absorb flavours.

Heat grill. Place kebabs on grill rack and cook for 3-4 minutes. Turn kebabs over, scatter chilli, onion and lime slices over top and baste with any remaining marinade. Grill for a further 3-4 minutes, until fish flakes easily. Serve hot.

Serves 4.

Note: You can use other white fish fillets, such as sole or plaice, instead of monkfish.

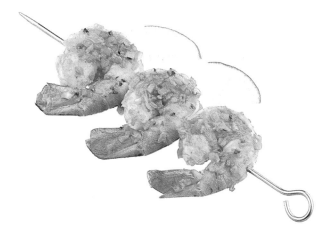

KING PRAWN KEBABS

12 raw Mediterranean (king) prawns
2 tablespoons vegetable oil
6 teaspoons lime juice
2 cloves garlic, crushed
½ teaspoon paprika
½ teaspoon turmeric
2 fresh green chillies, seeded and finely chopped
1 tablespoon chopped fresh coriander
lime slices, to garnish

Peel prawns, leaving tail shells on, then make a small incision along the spines and remove black vein. Thread onto skewers and set aside.

Whisk vegetable oil, lime juice, garlic, paprika and turmeric together. Stir in chillies. Put skewered prawns in a non-metal dish and spoon over marinade. Cover and leave in a cool place for 30 minutes, basting occasionally.

Heat grill. Drain skewered prawns and place on a grill rack. Cook for 3-5 minutes, turning and basting occasionally with the marinade, until just tender. Sprinkle with fresh coriander and serve hot, garnished with lime slices.

Serves 4.

COCONUT SPICED COD

four 185-250 g (6-8 oz) cod steaks
salt and pepper
2 tablespoons vegetable oil
1 onion, chopped
125 g (4 oz/1⅓ cups) desiccated coconut
5 cm (2 in) piece fresh root ginger, grated
2 cloves garlic, crushed
2 green chillies, seeded and chopped
½ teaspoon chilli powder
grated peel and juice of 1 lemon
2 tablespoons chopped fresh coriander
2 tomatoes, skinned, seeded and diced
oregano leaves, to garnish

Wash cod steaks and pat dry with absorbent kitchen paper. Place in a greased ovenproof dish and sprinkle with salt and pepper. Heat oil in a frying pan, add onion and fry, stirring, for about 5 minutes or until soft. Stir in coconut, ginger, garlic, chillies and chilli powder and fry, stirring, for 3-5 minutes, until golden brown.

Stir in lemon peel and juice and simmer, covered, for 10 minutes to soften coconut. Preheat oven to 160C (325F/Gas 3). Stir coriander and tomatoes into coconut mixture and spoon over cod steaks. Cook for 20-25 minutes, until fish flakes easily. Serve hot, garnished with oregano leaves.

Serves 4.

Note: Cover with foil during cooking if coconut begins to brown too much.

GRILLED SPICED FISH

four 250 g (8 oz) whole plaice or flounder, skinned
salt and pepper
155 ml (5 fl oz/²⁄₃ cup) natural yogurt
2 cloves garlic, crushed
2 teaspoons Garam Masala, see page 11
1 teaspoon ground coriander
½ teaspoon chilli powder
3 teaspoons lemon juice
lemon wedges and parsley sprigs, to garnish

Wash fish, pat dry with absorbent kitchen
paper and place in a shallow non-metal dish.
Sprinkle with salt and pepper.

Mix together yogurt, garlic, garam masala,
coriander, chilli powder and lemon juice.
Pour over fish and cover. Leave in a cool
place for 2-3 hours to allow fish to absorb
flavours.

Heat grill. Transfer fish to a grill rack and
cook for about 8 minutes, basting with
cooking juices and turning over halfway
through cooking, until fish flakes easily.
Serve hot, garnished with lemon wedges and
parsley sprigs.

Serves 4.

Note: Use fillets instead of whole fish, if
preferred, and grill for about 2 minutes less.

CARROT HALVA

625 g (1¼ lb) carrots, coarsely grated
750 ml (24 fl oz/3 cups) milk
8 green cardamom pods, bruised
60 ml (2 fl oz/¼ cup) vegetable oil
60 g (2 oz/¼ cup) caster sugar
30 g (1 oz/2 tablespoons) sultanas
60 g (2 oz/⅓ cup) shelled pistachio nuts, coarsely
    chopped
250 ml (8 fl oz/1 cup) strained Greek yogurt, to serve

Put carrots, milk and cardamom pods in a heavy-based saucepan and bring to the boil over a high heat.

Reduce the heat to medium and cook, uncovered, for about 50 minutes, stirring occasionally, until liquid has been absorbed. Heat oil in a large frying pan, add carrot mixture and fry, stirring constantly, for 10-15 minutes, until mixture turns a deep red colour.

Stir in sugar, sultanas and half the pistachios. Cook for 1-2 minutes more to heat through. Serve warm, topped with yogurt and sprinkled with remaining pistachio nuts.

Serves 6-8.

PISTACHIO HALVA

185 g (6 oz/1¼ cups) shelled pistachio nuts
250 ml (8 fl oz/1 cup) boiling water
2 tablespoons milk
125 g (4 oz/½ cup) sugar
22 g (¾ oz/4½ teaspoons) butter or ghee
few drops vanilla essence

Put pistachio nuts in a bowl, pour over boiling water and leave to soak for 30 minutes. Grease and base-line an 18 cm (7 in) square tin.

Drain pistachio nuts thoroughly and put in a blender or food processor fitted with a metal blade. Add milk and process until finely chopped, scraping mixture down from sides once or twice. Stir in sugar. Heat a large non-stick frying pan, add butter or ghee and melt over a low to medium heat. Add nut paste and cook for about 15 minutes, stirring constantly, until mixture is very thick.

Stir in vanilla essence, then spoon into prepared tin and spread evenly. Leave to cool completely, then cut into 20 squares using a sharp knife.

Makes about 20 squares.

Note: This halva will keep for 2-3 weeks, stored in the refrigerator.

FRITTERS & FRAGRANT SYRUP

500 g (1 lb/2 cups) caster sugar
5 green cardamom pods, bruised
1 teaspoon rosewater
pinch saffron threads
125 g (4 oz/1 cup) plain flour
3 teaspoons baking powder
185 g (6 oz/2⅓ cups) low-fat milk powder
15 g (½ oz/3 teaspoons) butter, melted
155 ml (5 fl oz/⅔ cup) natural yogurt
about 125 ml (4 fl oz/½ cup) milk
60 g (2 oz/⅓ cup) raisins
vegetable oil for frying
rose petals, to decorate

Put sugar and 500 ml (16 fl oz/2 cups) water in a heavy-based pan and heat gently, stirring occasionally, until sugar dissolves. Bring to the boil, then boil for about 5 minutes or until thickened and syrupy. Stir in cardamom pods, rosewater and saffron threads and keep warm. Meanwhile, sift flour and baking powder together into a mixing bowl and stir in milk powder. Mix in butter and yogurt and enough milk to make a soft dough.

With floured hands, divide dough into 24 pieces. Make a depression in centre of each and press in 2 or 3 raisins. Cover raisins with dough and roll into balls. Half-fill a deep-fat pan or fryer with oil and heat to 190C (375F). Fry 4 or 5 balls at a time, for 3-5 minutes, until a deep golden brown. Drain on absorbent kitchen paper, then add to the syrup. Serve hot, decorated with rose petals.

Serves 4-6.

CARDAMOM & NUT ICE CREAM

2 litres (3½ pints/8 cups) milk
12 green cardamom pods, bruised
90 g (3 oz/⅓ cup) caster sugar
45 g (1½ oz/⅓ cup) chopped blanched almonds,
** toasted**
45 g (1½ oz/⅓ cup) chopped pistachio nuts
mint sprigs, to decorate

Put milk and cardamom pods in a large heavy-based pan and bring to the boil. Reduce heat to medium-low and simmer, uncovered, stirring frequently, for 30 minutes or until milk is reduced by about two-thirds. Remove cardamom pods with a slotted spoon and discard.

Stir in sugar, almonds and half the pistachio nuts and simmer for 5 minutes more. Leave to cool. Pour reduced milk into a plastic container, cover and freeze for 2-3 hours, until frozen around edge. Spoon into a food processor fitted with a metal blade and process until smooth and light. Return to container, cover and freeze for 1 hour. Meanwhile, put 6 individual 185 ml (6 fl oz/ ¾ cup) moulds into freezer to chill.

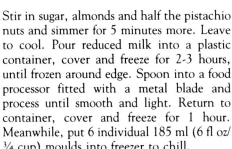

Spoon semi-frozen mixture into moulds, pressing down firmly. Cover and freeze for 2-3 hours, until solid. To serve, dip moulds in hot water for a few seconds and turn out onto plates. Serve at once, sprinkled with remaining pistachio nuts and decorated with mint sprigs.

Serves 6.

Note: If preferred, whisk ice cream with an electric whisk instead of a food processor.

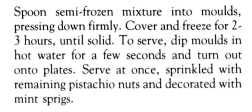

SAFFRON YOGURT

625 ml (20 fl oz/2½ cups) natural yogurt
pinch saffron threads
6 teaspoons boiling water
seeds from 6 cardamom pods
9 teaspoons caster sugar
lemon peel and cardamom seeds, to decorate

Pour yogurt into a nylon sieve lined with muslin and leave in refrigerator overnight to drain.

Put saffron and water in a small bowl and leave to soak for 30 minutes. Tip drained yogurt into a bowl and stir in saffron and its soaking liquid.

Put cardamom seeds in a mortar and crush lightly with a pestle. Stir into yogurt with sugar. Serve chilled, decorated with lemon peel and cardamom seeds.

Serves 4-6.

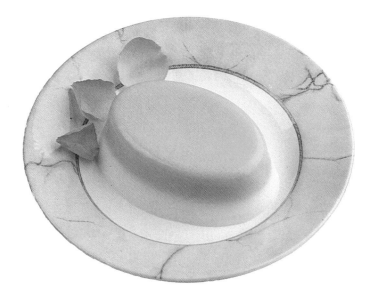

ROSEWATER PUDDING

3 teaspoons powdered gelatine
625 ml (20 fl oz/2½ cups) milk
9 teaspoons caster sugar
2 teaspoons rosewater
few drops red food colouring
pink rose petals, to decorate

Sprinkle gelatine over 9 teaspoons water in a small bowl and leave to soften for 2-3 minutes. Put milk in a separate saucepan and heat until almost boiling, then add gelatine and stir until dissolved completely. Stir in sugar and rosewater.

Pour half the mixture into a bowl, add a few drops red food colouring to colour it a delicate pink and whisk until cool and frothy. Wet four 185 ml (6 fl oz/¾ cup) individual moulds and divide pink mixture between them. Chill for about 30 minutes, until mixture is just set but still sticky on top. Meanwhile, keep remaining white mixture in a warm place to prevent it from setting. Whisk white mixture until frothy and pour into moulds on top of pink mixtures.

Chill until set, then dip moulds in hot water for 1-2 seconds and turn out onto plates. Serve cold, decorated with rose petals.

Serves 4.

Note: Before turning puddings out, wet serving plates with very little cold water. This prevents the moulds sticking to the plates, allowing you to move them to the centres, if necessary.

SAFFRON RICE PUDDING

185 g (6 oz/1¼ cups) basmati rice
75 ml (2½ fl oz/⅓ cup) milk
pinch saffron threads
30 g (1 oz/6 teaspoons) butter
2 green cardamom pods, bruised
2.5 cm (1 in) cinnamon stick
2 cloves
90 g (3 oz/½ cup) sultanas
60 g (2 oz/¼ cup) caster sugar
45 g (1½ oz/⅓ cup) flaked almonds, toasted

Wash rice under cold running water and put into a large saucepan with 625 ml (20 fl oz/2½ cups) cold water.

Bring to the boil, then reduce heat and simmer, covered, for 5 minutes. Drain. Measure 6 teaspoons milk into a small bowl, add saffron and leave to soak for 5 minutes. Melt butter in a heavy-based saucepan, add rice, cardamom pods, cinnamon and cloves and fry for 2-3 minutes or until rice becomes opaque.

Stir in milk, saffron milk, sultanas and sugar and bring to the boil, then simmer, covered, for 6-8 minutes, until rice is tender and liquid has been absorbed. Remove whole spices and serve hot, with flaked almonds scattered on top.

Serves 4.

COCONUT PANCAKES

125 g (4 oz/1 cup) plain flour
pinch salt
1 egg, beaten
about 315 ml (10 fl oz/1¼ cups) milk
45 g (1½ oz/9 teaspoons) demerara sugar
220 g (7 oz/4 cups) shredded fresh coconut
1 cm (½ in) piece fresh root ginger, grated
6 aniseeds, crushed
natural yogurt, to serve

Sift flour and salt together into a mixing bowl. Whisk in egg and half of the milk to make a smooth, thick batter.

Set batter aside in a cool place for 30 minutes, then stir in enough of remaining milk to make batter the consistency of single (light) cream. Heat a 15 cm (6 in) frying pan, brush with a little oil and pour in 2-3 tablespoons batter, tipping pan to coat base. Cook over a medium to high heat for 1-2 minutes, until browned, then flip pancake over with a palette knife and cook other side for about 30 seconds, until browned.

Turn pancake onto a plate and make 7 more pancakes in same way, stacking them on the plate as they are ready. In a small bowl, mix together sugar, 185 g (6 oz/3⅔ cups) coconut, ginger and aniseed. Spread a spoonful of mixture on each pancake and fold into quarters. Cover and chill for about 30 minutes. Decorate with remaining coconut sprinkled over tops, and serve cold with yogurt.

Serves 4.

GOLDEN SEMOLINA PUDDING

125 g (4 oz/½ cup) caster sugar
45 g (1½ oz/9 teaspoons) butter or ghee
125 g (4 oz/¾ cup) semolina
seeds from 3 cardamom pods
30 g (1 oz/¼ cup) raisins
60 g (2 oz/½ cup) flaked almonds, toasted

Put sugar in a heavy-based saucepan with 155 ml (5 fl oz/⅔ cup) water. Cook over a low heat, stirring occasionally, until sugar has dissolved. Bring to the boil and boil for 1 minute, then remove from heat and set aside.

Melt butter or ghee in a large heavy-based frying pan, add semolina and cook for 8-10 minutes over a medium heat, stirring constantly, until semolina turns golden brown.

Remove from heat and leave to cool slightly, then stir in sugar syrup and cardamom seeds. Cook over a low heat for 3-5 minutes, stirring frequently, until thick. Stir in half the raisins and almonds. Serve warm, decorated with remaining raisins and almonds.

Serves 4-6.

Note: Serve with natural yogurt, if desired.

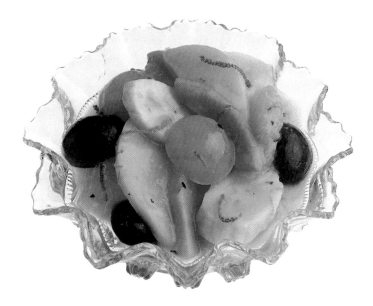

INDIAN FRUIT SALAD

2 mangoes
2 bananas
2 oranges
60 g (2 oz) black grapes
60 g (2 oz) green grapes
1 papaya (paw paw)
grated peel and juice of 1 lime
60 g (2 oz/¼ cup) caster sugar
freshly ground black pepper
natural yogurt, to serve

Peel and stone mangoes and cut flesh into thin slices, reserving any scraps. Peel and diagonally slice bananas.

Peel and segment oranges, working over a bowl to catch juices. Halve and pip both black and green grapes. Peel and halve papaya (paw paw), scoop out seeds and cut flesh into slices, reserving any scraps. Put fruit in a serving bowl and stir to combine.

Put orange juice, lime juice, sugar and scraps of mango and papaya (paw paw) in a blender or food processor fitted with a metal blade and process until smooth. Add lime peel and pepper. Pour over fruit and chill for at least 1 hour before serving with yogurt.

Serves 4-6.

Note: Use other fruits, such as melon, guava or pineapple, if preferred.

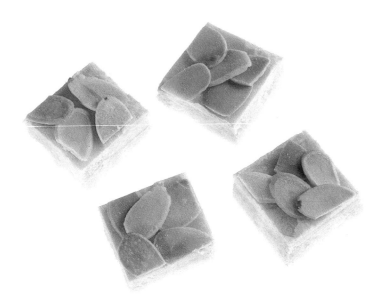

— TOASTED ALMOND TOFFEE —

500 g (1 lb/2 cups) sugar
155 g (5 oz/2 cups) low-fat milk powder
few drops vanilla essence
30 g (1 oz/¼ cup) flaked almonds, toasted

Grease and base-line an 18 cm (7 in) square tin. Put sugar in a large heavy-based saucepan with 250 ml (8 fl oz/1 cup) water and heat gently, stirring occasionally, until sugar is dissolved.

Bring to the boil, then boil over a medium-high heat until a few drops of mixture will form a soft ball in cold water. Stir in milk powder and cook for 3-4 minutes more, stirring constantly, until mixture begins to dry on spoon. Stir in vanilla.

Pour into prepared tin and spread evenly. Scatter almonds over top and press into surface. Leave to cool slightly, then cut into 25 squares with a sharp knife while still warm. Leave in tin until cold and firm.

Makes 25 squares.

—— COCONUT LAYER CAKE ——

60 g (2 oz/½ cup) plain flour
440 ml (14 fl oz/1⅔ cups) Coconut Milk, see page 11
6 egg yolks, beaten
125 g (4 oz/½ cup) caster sugar
seeds from 4 green cardamom pods, crushed
pinch freshly grated nutmeg
125 g (4 oz/½ cup) butter, melted
natural yogurt and slices of banana, to serve

Put flour in a mixing bowl, whisk in coconut milk, egg yolks, sugar, cardamom seeds and nutmeg, then leave batter to stand for 30 minutes.

Preheat oven to 220C (425F/Gas 7). Butter and base-line a 15 cm (6 in) soufflé dish. Add 3 teaspoons butter to dish and heat in oven for 5 minutes. Pour in one-seventh (5-6 tablespoons) of batter and bake for 10-15 minutes, until firm to touch and lightly browned. Continue adding another 3 layers, brushing cooked layer with butter before adding batter, then cooking each layer for 10-15 minutes.

Put soufflé dish in a roasting tin half-filled with boiling water, then continue adding final 3 layers in same way as before. When last layer is cooked, remove dish from oven and leave to cool. Run a knife around edge of dish to loosen cake and turn out onto a serving plate. Serve warm, with yogurt and sliced bananas.

Serves 4-6.

APRICOT DESSERT

250 g (8 oz/1¾ cups) ready-to-eat dried apricots
250 g (8 oz/1 cup) caster sugar
250 ml (8 fl oz/1 cup) whipping cream
60 g (2 oz/⅓ cup) blanched almonds, chopped and
   toasted

Put apricots in a saucepan with 250 ml (8 fl oz/1 cup) water and bring to the boil, then simmer, covered, for about 25 minutes or until very soft.

Meanwhile, put sugar and 500 ml (16 fl oz/2 cups) water in a heavy-based saucepan and heat gently, stirring occasionally, until sugar has dissolved. Bring to the boil and boil for 3 minutes or until syrupy. Drain apricots and purée in a blender or food processor fitted with a metal blade. Add syrup and process again.

Pour mixture into a bowl and leave to cool, then chill for at least 1 hour. Whip cream until holding soft peaks, fold half into apricot purée, leaving it slightly marbled, and spoon into serving dishes. Chill for 30 minutes, then top with remaining cream and scatter with chopped almonds.

Serves 4-6.

CASHEW NUT FUDGE

250 g (8 oz/1½ cups) unsalted cashew nuts
375 ml (12 fl oz/1½ cups) boiling water
6 teaspoons milk
155 g (5 oz/⅔ cup) sugar
15 g (½ oz/3 teaspoons) butter or ghee
few drops vanilla essence
few sheets silver leaf, see page 17

Put cashew nuts in a bowl, pour over boiling water and leave to soak for 1 hour. Grease and base-line an 18 cm (7 in) square tin.

Drain cashew nuts thoroughly and put in a blender or food processor fitted with a metal blade. Add milk and process until smooth, scraping mixture down from sides once or twice. Stir in sugar. Heat a large non-stick frying pan, add butter or ghee and melt over a low to medium heat. Add nut paste and cook for about 20 minutes, stirring constantly, until mixture is very thick.

Stir in vanilla essence, then spoon into prepared tin and spread evenly. Leave to cool completely, then press silver leaf onto surface. Cut fudge into about 25 diamond shapes using a wet sharp knife.

Makes about 25 pieces.

Note: This fudge will keep for 2-3 weeks if stored in an airtight tin.

FRESH MANGO CHUTNEY

2 mangoes
1 red chilli, seeded and finely sliced
30 g (1 oz/¼ cup) cashew nuts, chopped
30 g (1 oz/¼ cup) raisins
2 tablespoons chopped fresh mint
pinch asafoetida
½ teaspoon ground cumin
¼ teaspoon cayenne pepper
½ teaspoon ground coriander
mint sprigs, to garnish

Peel and stone mangoes, then very thinly slice flesh.

Put mango slices in a bowl with chilli, cashew nuts, raisins and mint and stir gently. In a small bowl, mix asafoetida, cumin, cayenne and coriander together, then sprinkle over mango mixture.

Stir gently to coat mango mixture in spices, then cover and chill for 2 hours. Serve chilled, garnished with mint sprigs.

Makes about 250 g (8 oz).

LIME PICKLE

12 limes
60 g (2 oz/¼ cup) coarse sea salt
3 teaspoons fenugreek seeds
3 teaspoons mustard seeds
6 teaspoons chilli powder
3 teaspoons ground turmeric
250 ml (8 fl oz/1 cup) vegetable oil, such as sunflower
   or peanut
coriander sprigs, to garnish

Cut each lime lengthwise into 8 thin wedges. Place in a large sterilised bowl, sprinkle with salt and set aside.

Put fenugreek and mustard seeds in a frying pan and dry roast them over a medium heat for 1-2 minutes, until they begin to pop. Put them in a mortar and grind them to a fine powder with a pestle.

Add chilli powder and turmeric and mix well. Sprinkle spice mixture over limes and stir. Pour over oil and cover with a dry cloth. Leave in a sunny place for 10-12 days, until softened. Pack into sterilised jars, then seal and store in a cool, dark place. It can be kept for 1-2 weeks. Serve at room temperature, garnished with coriander.

Makes about 1.5 kg (3 lb).

Variation: To make Lemon Pickle, substitute 8 lemons for the limes.

FRESH MINT RELISH

250 g (8 oz) fresh mint leaves, finely chopped
3 fresh green chillies, seeded and finely chopped
1 small onion, finely chopped
2.5 cm (1 in) piece fresh root ginger, finely chopped
salt
2 teaspoons caster sugar
6 teaspoons lemon juice
mint leaves and lemon slices, to garnish

Put chopped mint leaves, chillies, onion and ginger in a bowl and mix thoroughly. Cover and chill for at least 1 hour.

Season with salt and stir in sugar and lemon juice, mixing well. Serve chilled, garnished with mint leaves and lemon slices.

Makes about 375 g (12 oz).

Variation: For a milder relish, omit green chillies and add 2 tablespoons chopped fresh coriander instead.

SAUTÉED CHILLI PICKLE

2 teaspoons sesame seeds
1 teaspoon fennel seeds
2 teaspoons coriander seeds
2 teaspoons cumin seeds
60 ml (2 fl oz/¼ cup) vegetable oil
½ teaspoon black peppercorns
20 fresh green chillies
1 teaspoon mango powder
9 teaspoons lemon juice
grated lemon peel, to garnish, if desired

Put sesame, fennel, coriander and cumin seeds in a frying pan. Dry roast over a medium heat until spices begin to pop.

Add oil, peppercorns, chillies and mango powder and fry, stirring, for 3-5 minutes or until chillies are softened. Transfer to a serving dish, sprinkle over lemon juice and leave to cool. Serve at room temperature, garnished with lemon peel, if desired.

Makes about 185 g (6 oz).

Note: For a less hot pickle, halve and seed chillies before frying.

— CORIANDER LEAF CHUTNEY —

juice of 2 lemons
45 g (1½ oz/1 cup) shredded fresh coconut
2.5 cm (1 in) piece fresh root ginger, grated
1 green chilli, seeded
125 g (4 oz) fresh coriander leaves
2 spring onions, chopped
2 teaspoons caster sugar
salt
coriander leaves and spring onion tassels, to garnish

Put lemon juice, coconut, ginger and chilli in a blender or food processor fitted with a metal blade and process until smooth. Spoon into a bowl.

Finely shred coriander leaves and stir into coconut mixture with spring onions and sugar. Season with salt. Cover and chill for at least 1 hour. Serve chilled, garnished with coriander and spring onion tassels.

Makes about 250 g (8 oz).

Note: If fresh coconut is unavailable, substitute the same quantity desiccated coconut, soaked in 75 ml (2½ fl oz/⅓ cup) boiling water for 10 minutes, then drained and squeezed dry.

AUBERGINE PICKLE

750 g (1½ lb) baby aubergines (eggplants)
½ teaspoon turmeric
salt
500 ml (16 fl oz/2 cups) vegetable oil
6 cloves garlic, crushed
2.5 cm (1 in) piece fresh root ginger, grated
3 teaspoons Garam Masala, see page 11
1 teaspoon cayenne pepper

Cut aubergines (eggplants) in half lengthwise and sprinkle with turmeric and salt.

Heat 75 ml (2½ fl oz/⅓ cup) oil in a large frying pan and fry aubergines (eggplants) for about 5 minutes, stirring frequently, until golden brown. Stir in garlic and ginger and fry for 2 minutes. Stir in garam masala, cayenne pepper and remaining oil and cook, uncovered, for 10-15 minutes, stirring occasionally, or until aubergines are soft.

Leave to cool, then spoon into sterilised jars. Cover jars with a dry cloth and leave in a sunny place for 3 days, stirring gently every day. Seal jars and store in a cool, dark place for up to 2 months. Serve the pickle at room temperature.

Makes about 750 g (1½ lb).

Note: If baby aubergines (eggplants) are unavailable, use larger ones and quarter lengthwise, then slice and prepare as above.

CUCUMBER RAITA

⅓ cucumber
250 ml (8 fl oz/1 cup) natural yogurt
1 tablespoon chopped fresh coriander
1 tablespoon chopped fresh mint
1 green chilli, seeded and finely chopped
salt
1 teaspoon cumin seeds
1 teaspoon mustard seeds
coriander or mint leaves, to garnish

Cut cucumber into 0.3 cm x 1 cm (⅛ x ½ in) sticks and place in a bowl.

Add yogurt, coriander, mint and chilli and stir gently to mix. Season with salt. Chill for 30 minutes.

Meanwhile, put cumin and mustard seeds in a frying pan and dry roast them over a medium heat for 1-2 minutes, until they begin to pop. Leave to cool, then sprinkle over the yogurt mixture. Serve chilled, garnished with coriander or mint leaves.

Makes about 375 ml (12 fl oz/1½ cups).

CARROT & PISTACHIO RAITA

30 g (1 oz/¼ cup) coarsely chopped pistachio nuts
60 g (2 oz/⅓ cup) raisins
90 ml (3 fl oz/⅓ cup) boiling water
4 carrots, coarsely grated
185 ml (6 fl oz/¾ cup) natural yogurt
1 tablespoon chopped fresh mint
½ teaspoon chilli powder
½ teaspoon cardamom seeds, crushed
½ teaspoon ground cumin
salt

Put pistachio nuts and raisins in a small bowl and pour over boiling water. Leave to soak for 30 minutes, then drain and pat dry with absorbent kitchen paper.

Put carrots, yogurt, chopped mint, chilli powder, cardamom seeds and cumin in a bowl, season with salt and stir to mix.

Chill for 30 minutes. Stir all but 2 tablespoons pistachio nuts and raisins into yogurt, then sprinkle remainder on top. Serve the raita chilled.

Makes about 375 ml (12 fl oz/1½ cups).

Variation: Substitute chopped blanched almonds for pistachio nuts.

BEETROOT & YOGURT SALAD

6 cooked baby beetroots
250 ml (8 fl oz/1 cup) natural yogurt
1 teaspoon sugar
salt and cayenne pepper
1 tablespoon snipped fresh chives
small bunch of chives, to garnish

Cut beetroot into 0.3 cm (⅛ in) thick slices and arrange on a serving plate. Cover and chill for 30 minutes.

Put yogurt into a bowl and stir in sugar, then season with salt and cayenne pepper. Chill for 30 minutes.

Pour yogurt mixture over beetroot and sprinkle with snipped chives. Serve chilled, garnished with chives.

Serves 4-6.

Variation: Cut beetroot into tiny dice and stir into yogurt before chilling.

CUCUMBER & CHILLIES

250 g (8 oz) cucumber
salt
2 fresh green chillies, seeded and finely sliced, see
  Note
1 small fresh red chilli, seeded and finely chopped
½ teaspoon onion seeds
6 teaspoons white wine vinegar
1 teaspoon caster sugar

Very thinly slice the cucumber.

Place the cucumber slices in a colander and sprinkle with plenty of salt. Leave to drain for 30 minutes, then rinse thoroughly under cold running water. Pat dry with absorbent kitchen paper and arrange on a serving plate.

In a small bowl, mix together chillies and onion seeds and sprinkle over cucumber. Put vinegar and sugar in a bowl and mix well. Sprinkle over cucumber, then cover and chill for 30 minutes. Serve chilled.

Serves 4-6.

Note: The seeds of chillies can be left in, if preferred, to make the dish very hot.

TOMATO KUCHUMBER

375 g (12 oz) cherry tomatoes
6 spring onions
1 green chilli, seeded and chopped
3 teaspoons lemon juice
2 tablespoons chopped fresh coriander
salt and cayenne pepper
spring onion tassels, to garnish, if desired

Quarter the cherry tomatoes and arrange them in a serving bowl.

Cut spring onions diagonally into long, thin slices. Scatter onions and chilli over tomatoes and gently mix together.

Sprinkle vegetables with lemon juice and coriander and season with salt and cayenne pepper, then cover and chill for 30 minutes. Serve chilled, garnished with spring onion tassels, if desired.

Serves 4-6.

Variation: Use larger tomatoes, if preferred: slice thinly and arrange on a serving plate. Scatter other ingredients over top before chilling.

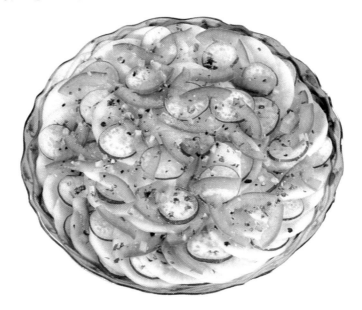

– WHITE & RED RADISH SALAD –

185 g (6 oz) white radish (mooli)
10 red radishes
1 small green pepper (capsicum)
1 fresh green chilli, seeded and finely chopped
6 teaspoons lime juice
salt
6 black peppercorns, coarsely ground
1 tablespoon chopped fresh mint

Peel and thinly slice white radish and slice red radishes. Arrange on a serving plate.

Cut pepper (capsicum) into 6 lengthwise, remove seeds and stalk and slice finely. Scatter pepper (capsicum) and chilli over radishes.

Sprinkle salad with lime juice, salt, peppercorns and mint. Cover and chill for 30 minutes. Serve chilled.

Serves 4-6.

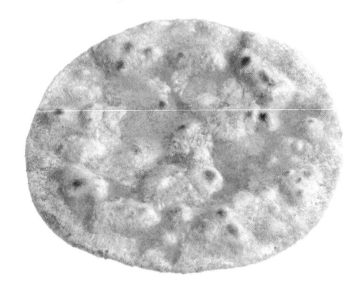

CHAPATI

155 g (5 oz/1¼ cups) plain flour
155 g (5 oz/1¼ cups) wholewheat flour
salt
60 g (2 oz/¼ cup) butter or ghee, melted, for serving

Sift flours and salt together into a mixing bowl and tip in any bran caught in sieve. Mix in about 185 ml (6 fl oz/¾ cup) water to make a soft dough.

Knead dough on a lightly floured surface for about 5 minutes, until smooth and pliable, then, with wet hands, knead dough for 1 minute more to make it extra smooth. Wrap in plastic wrap and chill for 30 minutes. Divide dough into 12 pieces and roll each out on a lightly floured surface to a 12.5 cm (5 in) round.

Heat a griddle or heavy-based frying pan on a medium heat and cook dough rounds, 1 at a time, floury side down, for 1-2 minutes, until beginning to bubble on surface. Turn over and cook second side for ½-1 minute, pressing with a folded dry cloth during cooking to make them puff up. Wrap each chapati in a dry cloth as soon as it is ready. Serve them warm, brushed with melted butter or ghee.

Makes 12.

NAAN

500 g (1 lb/4 cups) plain flour
1 teaspoon baking powder
½ teaspoon bicarbonate of soda
salt
1 egg, beaten
6 tablespoons natural yogurt
45 g (1½ oz/9 teaspoons) butter or ghee, melted
about 250 ml (8 fl oz/1 cup) milk
3 teaspoons poppy seeds

Sift flour, baking powder and bicarbonate of soda together into a mixing bowl. Season with salt.

Stir in egg, yogurt and 30 g (1 oz/6 teaspoons) butter or ghee. Gradually mix in enough milk to make a soft dough. Cover bowl with a damp cloth and put in a warm place for 2 hours. Preheat oven to 200C (400F/Gas 6). Knead dough on a lightly floured surface for 2-3 minutes, until smooth, then divide dough into 8 pieces.

Roll each piece into a ball, then roll out to make ovals about 15 cm (6 in) long, pulling ends to stretch dough into shape. Brush ovals with water and place wet-side down on greased baking trays. Brush dry side with melted butter or ghee and sprinkle with poppy seeds. Bake for 8-10 minutes, until puffy and golden brown. Serve at once.

Makes 8.

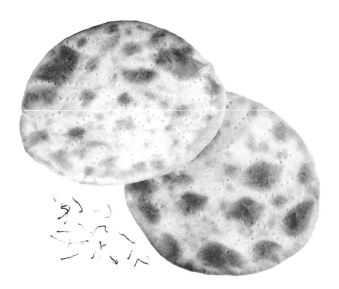

FLAKY OVEN BREAD

500 g (1 lb/4 cups) plain flour
salt
125 g (4 oz/½ cup) butter or ghee
2 teaspoons caster sugar
about 500 ml (16 fl oz/2 cups) milk
pinch saffron threads

Sift flour and salt to taste together into a mixing bowl. Rub in all but 15 g (½ oz/3 teaspoons) of the butter or ghee until mixture resembles breadcrumbs. Stir in sugar, then add about 315 ml (10 fl oz/1¼ cups) milk to make a soft dough.

Knead dough until smooth, then put in a clean, lightly oiled bowl. Cover and leave in a cool place for 2 hours. Put remaining milk in a small pan and heat until almost boiling, add saffron threads and leave to soak for 1½-2 hours. Preheat oven to 230C (450F/Gas 8) and place a heavy baking tray in oven to heat. Knead dough on a lightly floured surface and divide into 8 pieces. Roll 4 pieces at a time into balls, keeping rest covered with a dry cloth.

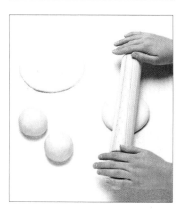

Flatten and roll first 4 balls out to 15 cm (6 in) rounds. Prick all over with a fork. Press onto heated baking tray in oven and bake for about 8 minutes, until beginning to brown, sprinkling rounds with a little saffron milk twice without removing them from oven. Melt remaining butter or ghee and brush over breads, then stack them buttered-sides together and wrap in a dry cloth while preparing remaining rounds. Serve warm.

Makes 8.

PARATHA

250 g (8 oz/2 cups) plain flour
250 g (8 oz/2 cups) wholewheat flour
salt
½ teaspoon onion seeds
½ teaspoon celery seeds
250 g (8 oz/1 cup) butter or ghee, melted
celery leaves, to garnish

Sift flours and salt to taste together into a mixing bowl and tip in any bran caught in the sieve. Stir in onion and celery seeds, then mix in about 155 ml (5 fl oz/⅔ cup) water to form a fairly soft dough.

Knead dough on a lightly floured surface for 5 minutes or until pliable and smooth. Wrap in plastic wrap and chill for 30 minutes. Divide dough into 10 pieces and roll each out to a 12.5 cm (5 in) round. Brush 1 side of each round with butter or ghee, then fold in half with buttered side inside. Brush top side with butter and fold in half again to make a triangle.

Roll out on a lightly floured surface until straight sides measure about 12.5 cm (5 in). Heat a griddle or heavy-based frying pan and brush with butter or ghee. Cook 2 or 3 at a time for 1 minute, then brush with butter, turn over and cook 1-2 minutes more. Stack on a plate and cover with a cloth while cooking remainder. Serve warm, garnished with celery leaves.

Makes 10.

POORI

45 g (1½ oz/⅓ cup) plain flour
45 g (1½ oz/⅓ cup) wholewheat flour
pinch salt
¼ teaspoon cardamom seeds
about 2 tablespoons vegetable oil plus extra for deep frying
about 60 ml (2 fl oz/¼ cup) warm water

Sift flours and salt together into a mixing bowl and tip in any bran caught in sieve. Stir in cardamom seeds and 3 teaspoons oil and mix in enough of the water to make a soft dough.

Knead dough for 5 minutes on a lightly oiled surface with a little oil rubbed into hands to prevent them sticking until dough is soft and pliable. Cover with plastic wrap and leave to rest for 10 minutes. Divide dough into 8 pieces and roll into balls. Dust balls with flour and cover with a damp cloth. Roll each ball out to a 7.5 cm (3 in) round, keeping unrolled balls and finished rounds covered with the cloth.

Half-fill a deep-fat pan or fryer with oil and heat to 190C (375F) or until a day-old cube of bread browns in 40 seconds. Fry poori 1 at a time, turning over once, for ½-1 minute, until golden. Keep patting top of each poori gently with a slotted spoon as it cooks to make it puff up. Serve at once.

Makes 8.

DOSA

60 g (2 oz/⅓ cup) urad dhal (mung beans, split not
  husked)
155 g (5 oz/1 cup) long-grain rice
2 spring onions, finely chopped
2 tablespoons chopped fresh coriander
2.5 cm (1 in) piece fresh root ginger, grated
1 fresh green chilli, seeded and chopped
½ teaspoon salt
about 3 tablespoons vegetable oil
coriander leaves, to garnish

Wash dhal and rice thoroughly and put into
separate bowls. Add 500 ml (16 fl oz/2 cups)
water to each and leave to soak for 3 hours,
then drain well.

Put dhal in a blender or food processor fitted
with a metal blade. Add 90 ml (3 fl oz/⅓
cup) water and process until smooth. Purée
rice with 90 ml (3 fl oz/ ⅓ cup) water in
same way. Mix purées together in a large
bowl, cover with a damp cloth and set aside
at room temperature for about 12 hours.

Stir in onions, coriander, ginger, chilli, salt
and about 9 teaspoons water to make a
batter. Heat a 15 cm (6 in) frying pan, brush
with a little oil, then spoon in 2-3 tablespoons batter and spread into a 10 cm (4 in)
circle. Cook over a high heat for about 3
minutes, turning over with a fish slice after
half the time, until browned. Cover with a
dry cloth while cooking remainder. Serve
warm, garnished with coriander leaves.

Makes about 12.

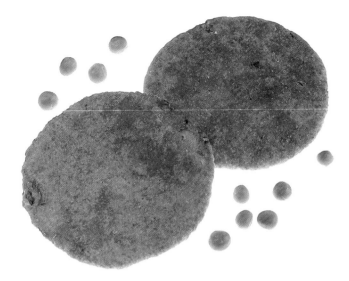

GREEN PEA KACHORI

250 g (8 oz/1¾ cups) wholewheat flour
¼ teaspoon salt
½ teaspoon cumin seeds
½ teaspoon aniseeds
6 teaspoons vegetable oil plus extra for deep frying
1 fresh green chilli, seeded and chopped
2.5 cm (1 in) piece fresh root ginger, grated
60 g (2 oz) frozen peas, thawed

Sift flour and salt together into a mixing bowl and tip in any bran caught in sieve. Mix in about 60 ml (2 fl oz/¼ cup) water to make a soft dough. Knead on a lightly floured surface for 5 minutes.

Set dough aside, covered with a dry cloth. Heat a frying pan, add cumin seeds and aniseeds and dry fry for ½-1 minute, until beginning to pop, then grind with a mortar and pestle. Heat oil in pan, add ground spices, chilli and ginger and fry for 2 minutes. Mash peas, then add to pan and cook for 1 minute more. Leave to cool, then divide dough into 12 pieces and roll into balls.

Make a depression in each dough ball, press in about 1 teaspoon filling and smooth over dough to seal. Roll each ball out on a lightly floured surface to a 7.5 cm (3 in) round. Half-fill a deep-fat pan or fryer with oil and heat to 190C (375F) or until a cube of day-old bread browns in 40 seconds. Fry 2 kachori at a time for 2-3 minutes or until golden brown. Serve warm.

Makes 12.

NIMKI

125 g (4 oz/1 cup) plain flour
½ teaspoon salt
15 g (½ oz/3 teaspoons) butter or ghee
large pinch chilli powder
¼ teaspoon caster sugar
½ teaspoon onion seeds
vegetable oil for deep frying
chilli flowers, to garnish, if desired

Sift flour and salt together into a mixing bowl, then rub in butter or ghee until mixture resembles breadcrumbs.

Stir in chilli powder, caster sugar and onion seeds, then mix in about 60 ml (2 fl oz/¼ cup) water to make a soft dough. Roll out dough on a floured surface to a thickness of 0.3 cm (⅛ in). Prick all over with a fork and cut into 2.5 cm (1 in) strips. Cut strips diagonally to make about 30 diamond shapes.

Half-fill a deep-fat pan or fryer with oil and heat to 190C (375F) or until a cube of day-old bread browns in 40 seconds. Fry nimki in 2 or 3 batches for 1-2 minutes each, until crisp and golden brown. Drain well and cool. Serve garnished with chilli flowers, if desired.

Makes about 30.

Note: These tiny crisp breads are ideal for party nibbles. Make 2 days ahead and store in an airtight tin.

BANANA YOGURT MILK SHAKE

4 ripe bananas
90 g (3 oz/⅓ cup) light soft brown sugar
1 teaspoon cardamom seeds
940 ml (30 fl oz/3¾ cups) cold milk
155 ml (5 fl oz/⅔ cup) natural yogurt
6 ice cubes

Peel and slice bananas and reserve a few slices for decoration.

Put remainder in a blender or food processor fitted with a metal blade with sugar, cardamom seeds, milk, yogurt and ice cubes. Process until smooth and very frothy.

Pour into tall glasses and decorate with reserved banana slices. Serve at once with wide straws.

Makes about 1.2 litres (2 pints/5 cups).

MILK & SAFFRON SHERBET

½ teaspoon saffron threads
6 teaspoons boiling water
90 g (3 oz/¾ cup) shelled pistachio nuts
seeds from 10 green cardamom pods
60 g (2 oz/¼ cup) caster sugar
1.2 litres (2 pints/5 cups) cold milk
crushed ice

Put saffron and boiling water in a small bowl and leave to soak for 30 minutes.

Put saffron and water in a blender or food processor with two-thirds pistachio nuts, cardamom seeds and sugar. Process until smooth. Add milk and process until frothy. Chop remaining nuts.

Half-fill glasses with ice and pour in frothy milk. Sprinkle with remaining pistachio nuts and serve at once.

Makes about 1.2 litres (2 pints/5 cups).

ORANGE SHERBET

about 8 oranges
125 g (4 oz/½ cup) caster sugar
ice cubes
625 ml (20 fl oz/2½ cups) sparkling mineral water
orange peel spirals and mint sprigs, to decorate

Squeeze juice from oranges to make 625 ml (20 fl oz/2½ cups) juice.

Meanwhile, put sugar and 625 ml (20 fl oz/ 2½ cups) water in a large saucepan and cook over a low heat, stirring occasionally, until sugar has dissolved. Bring to the boil and boil gently, uncovered, for 5 minutes. Add orange juice and boil gently for a further 5 minutes. Leave to cool, then chill.

To serve, put ice cubes in glasses, add a little orange syrup, top up with mineral water and decorate the glasses with orange peel spirals and mint sprigs.

Makes about 1.2 litres (2 pints/5 cups).

Note: Use ready-made freshly squeezed orange juice, if preferred.

MANGO MILK SHAKE

4 ripe mangoes
90 g (3 oz/⅓ cup) caster sugar
940 ml (30 fl oz/3¾ cups) cold milk
crushed ice

Peel and stone mangoes.

Put flesh in a blender or food processor fitted with a metal blade and process until smooth. Add sugar and milk and process until frothy.

Half-fill glasses with crushed ice and pour over mango milk shake. Serve at once, with wide straws.

Makes about 1.2 litres (2 pints/5 cups).

Note: If your blender or processor is small, process the milk shake in 2 batches.

— FRAGRANT LEMON SHERBET —

grated peel and juice of 2 lemons
60 g (2 oz/¼ cup) caster sugar
handful lemon balm leaves
crushed ice
about 1 litre (32 fl oz/4 cups) iced water
spirals of lemon peel and lemon balm leaves, to
**   decorate, see Note**

Put lemon peel and juice, sugar and lemon balm leaves in a blender or food processor and process until smooth. Strain into a jug and chill.

Fill glasses with crushed ice, pour over a little lemon concentrate and top up with iced water. Serve, decorated with spirals of lemon peel and lemon balm leaves.

Makes about 1.2 litres (2 pints/5 cups).

Note: To make lemon spiral decoration, cut a long strip of peel using a cannelle knife. Wind round a skewer or chopstick, fasten securely and blanch in boiling water for a few seconds. Rinse in cold water and remove skewer or chopstick.

SPICED TEA

5 teaspoons black peppercorns
3 teaspoons cardamom seeds
3 teaspoons cloves
4 cm (1½ in) cinnamon stick
30 g (1 oz/⅓ cup) ground ginger
Indian tea leaves
boiling water
sugar and milk, to taste

Put peppercorns, cardamom seeds, cloves and cinnamon in a mortar and grind to a fine powder with a pestle. Add ginger and grind again for a few seconds to mix.

Make a pot of tea and add about ½ tablespoon of spice mixture and leave in a warm place for 1-2 minutes to brew. Serve hot, with sugar and milk.

Makes about 8 tablespoons spice mix, enough for 16 pots tea.

Note: Store remaining spice mixture in a screw-topped jar in a dark cupboard to preserve its flavour. It will keep for 2-3 months.

LIME & MINT SHERBET

4-6 limes
60 g (2 oz/¼ cup) caster sugar
pinch salt
handful mint leaves
ice cubes
about 1 litre (32 fl oz/4 cups) iced water
mint leaves and lime slices, to decorate

Squeeze enough limes to make 90 ml (3 fl oz/
⅓ cup) juice.

Put the juice in a blender or food processor
fitted with a metal blade. Add sugar, salt
and mint leaves and process until smooth.
Strain into a jug, then chill.

Half-fill tall glasses with ice cubes, add a
little lime juice concentrate and top up with
iced water. Serve at once, decorated with
mint leaves and lime slices.

Makes about 1.2 litres (2 pints/5 cups).

— INDIAN SUMMER PUNCH —

3 teaspoons fennel seeds
seeds from 6 green cardamom pods
3 cloves
4 black peppercorns
60 g (2 oz/½ cup) ground almonds
30 g (1 oz/¼ cup) shelled pistachio nuts
60 g (2 oz/½ cup) sunflower seeds
315 ml (10 fl oz/1¼ cups) boiling water
125 g (4 oz/½ cup) caster sugar
940 ml (30 fl oz/3¾ cups) cold milk
apple slices and fennel sprigs, to decorate

Put fennel and cardamom seeds, cloves and peppercorns in a mortar and grind to a fine powder with a pestle.

Put almonds, pistachios and sunflower seeds in a small bowl and pour over 90 ml (3 fl oz/ ⅓ cup) boiling water. Leave to soak for 20 minutes, then drain. Put in a blender or food processor fitted with a metal blade and add remaining water and process until smooth.

Add spices and sugar and process again. Strain through a cloth or 2 layers of muslin, squeezing paste to extract as much liquid as possible. Discard paste and chill liquid for at least 1 hour, then mix with milk. Serve in tall glasses over ice, decorated with apple slices and fennel sprigs.

Makes about 1.9 litres (3 pints/7½ cups).

Note: If preferred, grind spices in a coffee grinder.

INDEX